McDougal, Littell
ENGLISH

Teacher's Edition
4
Aqua Level

Skills Practice Book

Green Level
Red Level
Gold Level
Silver Level
AQUA LEVEL
Brown Level
Plum Level
Pink Level

McDougal, Littell & Company

Evanston, Illinois

New York   Dallas   Sacramento   Raleigh

Special Features of This Skills Practice Book

- It contains hundreds of skill-building exercises in composition, vocabulary, grammar, usage, capitalization, and punctuation.

- Each page is a self-contained unit. It contains a brief explanation followed by comprehensive reinforcement exercises.

- Each page focuses on one—and only one—topic or skill.

- Key words and phrases are highlighted for greater clarity and ease of use.

- A comprehensive review lesson follows each major section of the text.

Acknowledgments

Atheneum Publishers, Inc.: For "Shadows," from *Catch Me a Wind* by Patricia Hubbell; copyright © 1968 by Patricia Hubbell. Bobbs-Merrill Co., Inc: For "Extremes" from *The Book of Joyous Children* by James Whitcomb Riley; copyright 1902, 1930 by James Whitcomb Riley. William Cole: For "If You Pinch a Dinosaur" by Shel Silverstein from *Dinosaurs and Beasts of Yore*, edited by William Cole and Ann K. Beneduce; copyright © 1979 by Shel Silverstein. Harper and Row Publishers, Inc.: For "Sleet Storm" from *A World to Know* by James S. Tippett; copyright 1933 by Harper and Brothers. Marci Ridlon McGill: For "I Never Win at Parties," from *That Was Summer* by Marci Ridlon; copyright © 1969 by Marci Ridlon. Marian Reiner: For "A Spark in the Sun. . . ." an original haiku from *Cricket Songs* Japanese haiku translated by Harry Behn; copyright © 1964 by Harry Behn. Ray Lincoln: For "Summer," from *Don't Ever Cross a Crocodile* by Kaye Starbird; copyright © 1963 by Kaye Starbird. Simon & Schuster, Inc.: For the dictionary excerpt reproduced on page 44, from *Webster's New World Dictionary for Young Readers;* copyright © 1976. Anne Tenney: For "Back and Forth" by Lucy Sprague Mitchell and "The Willows" by Walter Prichard Eaton from *Favorite Poems Old and New*, edited by Helen Ferris; copyright 1957; published by Doubleday and Co. World Book-Childcraft, International: For an excerpt from *The World Book Encyclopedia;* copyright © 1980 by World Book-Childcraft International, Inc. Every effort has been made to trace the ownership of all copyrighted material found in this book and to make full acknowledgment for its use. Portions of the material found in this book were previously published under the title *Building English Skills*, copyright by McDougal, Littell & Company.

Cover Art: *Flowers In The Summer* **by an elementary school student**

> **WARNING:** No part of this book may be reproduced or transmitted in any form or by any means, electronic or mechanical, including photocopying, recording, or by any information storage and retrieval system, without permission in writing from the Publisher. Any use of pages in this book contrary to the foregoing may constitute an infringement of copyright and is subject to all the penalties arising therefrom.

ISBN: 0-8123-5075-8   TE: 0-8123-5076-6

Copyright © 1987, 1984, 1981 by McDougal, Littell & Company
Box 1667, Evanston, Illinois 60204
All rights reserved. Printed in the United States of America

Contents

Discovering New Words
Context Clues: Definition and Restatement 1
Context Clues: Examples 2
Prefixes 3
Suffixes 4
Mixed Practice: Discovering New Words 5
Using Vocabulary in Writing 6
Review: Discovering New Words 7

Learning About Sentences
What Is a Sentence? 8
Kinds of Sentences (1) 9
Kinds of Sentences (2) 10
Parts of the Sentence 11
The Simple Subject 12
The Simple Predicate 13
Mixed Practice: Learning About Sentences 14
Using Sentences in Writing 15
Review: Learning About Sentences 16

Understanding Nouns
What Are Nouns? 17
Using Nouns as Subjects 18
Common and Proper Nouns 19
Singular and Plural Nouns 20
Making Nouns Show Possession 21
Mixed Practice: Understanding Nouns 22
Using Nouns in Writing 23
Review: Understanding Nouns 24

Understanding Verbs
Verbs That Tell About Action 25
Verbs That Say That Something Is 26
Main Verbs and Helping Verbs 27
Using Helping Verbs 28
Separated Parts of Verbs 29
Using the Right Form of *Be* 30
Using Contractions 31
Using Negatives Correctly 32
Mixed Practice (1): Understanding Verbs 33
Mixed Practice (2): Understanding Verbs 34
Using Verbs in Writing 35
Review: Understanding Verbs 36

Writing Better Sentences
Avoiding Sentence Fragments 37
Avoiding Run-on Sentences 38
Writing Compound Sentences 39
Using Sentences in Writing 40
Review: Writing Better Sentences 41

The Process of Writing a Paragraph
What Is a Paragraph? 42
The Topic Sentence 43
The Sentences in a Paragraph 44
Prewriting: Planning a Paragraph 45
Writing a Draft 46
Revising a Paragraph 47
Proofreading a Paragraph 48
Review: Writing a Paragraph 49

Managing Verb Forms
Verbs That Tell About Present Time 50
Verbs That Tell About the Past 51
Irregular Verbs 52
Mixed Practice: Managing Verb Forms 53
Using Verbs in Writing 54
Review: Managing Verb Forms 55

Writing a Narrative
Thinking About a Narrative 56
Prewriting: Planning a Narrative 57
Writing a Draft 58
Revising and Proofreading a Narrative 59
Review: Writing a Narrative 60

Understanding Adjectives
What Are Adjectives? 61
Three Kinds of Adjectives 62
Using *A*, *An*, and *The* 63
Using Adjectives To Compare 64
Mixed Practice: Understanding Adjectives 65
Using Adjectives in Writing 66
Review: Understanding Adjectives 67

Understanding Adverbs

What Are Adverbs? 68
Recognizing Adverbs 69
Making Comparisons with Adverbs 70
Mixed Practice: Understanding Adverbs 71
Using Adverbs in Writing 72
Review: Understanding Adverbs 73

Using the Dictionary and Thesaurus

Entry Words 74
Using Guide Words 75
Respelling and Pronunciation 76
Understanding the Definition 77
Synonyms and Antonyms 78
Using a Thesaurus 79
Mixed Practice: Using the Dictionary and Thesaurus 80
Using the Dictionary in Writing 81
Review: Using the Dictionary and Thesaurus 82

Writing a Description

Thinking About Descriptions 83
Prewriting: Selecting Details 84
Prewriting: Arranging Details 85
Writing a Draft 86
Revising and Proofreading a Description 87
Review: Writing a Description 88

Understanding Pronouns

What Are Pronouns? 89
Using Pronouns as Subjects 90
Using *Me, Us, Him, Her,* and *Them* 91
Using *I* and *Me, We* and *Us* Correctly 92
Possessive Pronouns 93
Using *Its, Your,* and *Their* 94
Mixed Practice: Understanding Pronouns 95
Using Pronouns in Writing 96
Review: Understanding Pronouns 97

Exploring the Library

Fiction Books 98
Nonfiction Books 99
Using the Card Catalog 100
Using Special Parts of a Book 101
Using an Encyclopedia 102
Review: Exploring the Library 103

Writing To Tell How

Thinking About Writing To Tell How 104
Prewriting: Planning To Tell How 105
Writing a Draft 106
Revising and Proofreading 107
Review: Writing To Tell How 108

Improving Speaking and Listening Skills

Making Announcements 109
Using the Telephone 110

Learning To Think Clearly

Understanding Fact and Opinion 111
Understanding Generalizations 112
Understanding Slanted Language 113
Review: Learning To Think Clearly 114

Writing To Explain an Opinion

Thinking About Opinions 115
Prewriting and Planning a Paragraph 116
Writing a Draft 117
Revising and Proofreading 118
Review: Writing To Explain an Opinion 119

Sharpening Study Skills

Learning Skills for Better Reading 120
Taking Notes from a Book 121
Taking Notes from an Encyclopedia 122
Taking Tests 123
Answering Test Questions 124
Review: Sharpening Study Skills 125

Writing a Report

Thinking About a Report 126
Prewriting: Choosing a Subject 127
Prewriting: Finding Information 128
Prewriting: Sorting Notes 129
Prewriting: Making an Outline 130
Writing a Draft 131
Revising a Report 132
Proofreading and Finishing a Report 133
Review: Writing a Report 134

Enjoying Poetry

The Speaker in Poems   135
Pictures in Poetry   136
Sound Patterns in Poetry   137
Rhythm in Poetry   138
Review: Enjoying Poetry   139

Using Capital Letters

Capitalizing Names of People and Pets   140
Capitalizing Names of Places and Things   141
Capitalizing First Words (1)   142
Capitalizing First Words (2)   143
Capitalizing Titles   144
Mixed Practice: Using Capital Letters   145
Using Capital Letters in Writing   146
Review: Using Capital Letters   147

Building Punctuation Power

The Period   148
The Question Mark   149
The Exclamation Point   150
The Comma (1)   151
The Comma (2)   152
The Comma (3)   153
The Apostrophe   154
Quotation Marks   155
Quotation Marks and Underlining in Titles   156
The Colon   157
Mixed Practice (1): Building Punctuation Power   158
Mixed Practice (2): Building Punctuation Power   159
Using Punctuation in Writing   160
Review: Building Punctuation Power   161

Writing Friendly Letters

The Parts of a Friendly Letter (1)   162
The Parts of a Friendly Letter (2)   163
Writing Invitations   164
Writing Thank-you Notes   165
Writing Business Letters (1)   166
Writing Business Letters (2)   167
Addressing the Envelope   168
Review: Writing Letters   169

Practice Pages on Irregular Verbs

Pretest: Using Irregular Verbs   170
Bring, Brought, Brought   171
Come, Came, Come   172
Do, Did, Done   173
Eat, Ate, Eaten   174
Give, Gave, Given   175
Go, Went, Gone   176
Run, Ran, Run   177
See, Saw, Seen   178
Take, Took, Taken   179
Throw, Threw, Thrown   180

Spelling

Adding Prefixes and Certain Suffixes   181
Words Ending in Silent *e* and *y*   182
Doubling the Final Consonant and Spelling Words with *ie* and *ei*   183

Context Clues: Definition and Restatement

Discovering New Words 1

When you find a new word in your reading, you find the word *in context*. **Context** is the sentence or the paragraph that new word is in. The context may give you the meaning of the new word. A **context clue** is a word or group of words that leads you to the meaning.

Sometimes a writer tells the meaning of a new word. He or she puts the *definition* or *restatement* of the new word in the context. Read the following examples.

The cowboy caught the horse with a lariat, that is, a long rope.

The desert is arid. In other words, it is dry and hot.

Bob plays lacrosse, a game played with balls and long-handled rackets.

The workman wore goggles—glasses to protect the eyes.

In each example, the writer defined the underlined word or restated it in other words.

These words or punctuation marks help you spot a definition or restatement in the context:

which is   that is   in other words   or
commas   dashes

Using Definition and Restatement Clues Each of these sentences has a context clue in it. The clue defines or restates the underlined word. Draw two lines under the words in each sentence that give the definition of the underlined word.

1. Bill was prompt, that is, on time.

2. We saw a gnu, a large African antelope, at the zoo.

3. Lydia's mother gave her a marionette, which is a puppet on strings.

4. The water was azure, or blue.

5. Mr. Key is an illustrator, in other words, a person who draws pictures.

6. Alice wants to be a physician—a doctor.

7. Joe's face showed great fatigue, that is, tiredness.

8. The fisherman threw out the grapnel—a small anchor with several prongs.

9. The copilot, the assistant to the pilot, was flying the plane.

10. In Europe you can visit many old cathedrals, or very large churches.

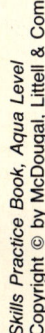

Context Clues: Examples

Discovering New Words
2

Another context clue that can help you find the meaning of new words is the use of examples. The writer may give examples of the new word. The examples list some things that are *like* the thing the new word describes. Look at these samples.

Mr. Tatman fixes appliances, like dishwashers and refrigerators.

Mrs. Muller raises fowl, such as chicken and ducks.

From these sentences, you can see that *appliances* are machines like dishwashers and refrigerators, and that *fowl* are animals such as chickens and ducks.

These words will help you spot example context clues:

| for example | especially | like |
| for instance | such as | |

Using Examples Each sentence below contains context clues that are examples. Draw two lines under the words that are examples of the underlined word.

1. When you have a fever, drink plenty of liquids, such as water and juice.
2. We get news from the media, for example, television and radio.
3. A family tree lists your ancestors, for instance, your parents, grandparents, and great-grandparents.
4. Cook the turkey giblets, especially the liver and gizzard, and add them to the gravy.
5. Precipitation, like rain, snow, or sleet, can be measured.

Using Context Clues Use the context clues in the sentences below to figure out the meaning of the underlined word. Draw two lines under the words that tell you the meaning. Look for definitions, restatements, and examples.

1. The sudden noise made Paul flinch, or pull back quickly.
2. The sailors made scrimshaw, which is carved whale bone.
3. Anita likes to embellish—decorate—her papers.
4. Vehicles, such as cars, trucks, and buses, must be inspected.
5. I read an anthology of fairy tales, that is, a collection of tales.

Prefixes

Discovering New Words
3

Many words that look new to you are built from words you already know. Sometimes they are made by adding a *prefix*. A **prefix** is a word part added to the front of a word. It changes the meaning of the word.

Here are four common prefixes.

un- This prefix means "not" or "the opposite of."
un + able = unable   *Unable* means "not able."
un + tie = untie   *Untie* means "the opposite of tie."

re- This prefix means "again" or "back."
re + load = reload   *Reload* means "load again."
re + pay = repay   *Repay* means "pay back."

mis- This prefix means "wrong" or "wrongly."
mis + use = misuse   *Misuse* means "use wrongly."

non- This prefix means "not."
non + voter = nonvoter   *Nonvoter* means "not a voter."

When you see a word that starts with one of these prefixes, break the word into two parts. You may know what the prefix means. You may know the meaning of the base word, or the word the prefix is added to. Put the two parts back together. Then you have the meaning of the new word.

Some words look as if they have prefixes, but they do not. Take off the letters you think make the prefix. If the word does not make sense, the word does not have a prefix. For example, you could not take *re* from *real; al* is not a word, so *re* is not a prefix.

Identifying Prefixes Underline the base word twice. Underline the prefix once. Write a meaning for the whole word.

EXAMPLE: uncut ____not cut____

1. remake ____make again____
2. nonfat ____not fat____
3. unbent ____not bent____
4. regain ____gain again____
5. misprint ____print wrongly____
6. unhurt ____not hurt____
7. nonequal ____not equal____
8. miscount ____count wrongly____

Suffixes

Discovering New Words 4

Sometimes a new word is made by adding a *suffix* to a base word. A **suffix** is a word part added to the end of a word. A suffix changes the meaning of the base word. Here are four common suffixes.

-er (*or* **-or**)   This suffix means "someone who does something."
   bake + er = baker   A *baker* is "someone who bakes."
   sail + or = sailor   A *sailor* is "someone who sails."

   The suffix *-er* can also mean *more*.
   rich + er = richer   *Richer* means "more rich."

-able   This suffix means "can be."
   move + able = movable   *Movable* means "can be moved."

-ful   This suffix means "full of."
   play + ful = playful   *Playful* means "full of play."

-less   This suffix means "without."
   fear + less = fearless   *Fearless* means "without fear."

Some words look as if they have suffixes, but they do not. When you take off the letters you think make the suffix, look at what is left. It must be a real word. If it is not a real word, you cannot break the word into parts. For example, you cannot break *table* into parts. *T* is not a word; so *able* is not a suffix.

Understanding Suffixes Underline the base word twice. Underline the suffix once. Write a meaning for the word.

   EXAMPLE: juggler   one who juggles

1. homeless   without a home
2. joyful   full of joy
3. teacher   someone who teaches
4. readable   can be read
5. returnable   can be returned
6. painter   someone who paints
7. penniless   without a penny
8. careful   full of care
9. stronger   more strong
10. stainless   without a stain

Mixed Practice: Discovering New Words

Discovering New Words 5

Finding Meanings of Words Each sentence below has an underlined word. The meaning of some of these words is given in a context clue. The meaning of other words can be found by looking at the prefixes and suffixes of the word. Write, in your own words, the meaning of the underlined word. Then tell whether you used **context** or **word parts** to find the meaning. **Wording of definitions may vary.**

1. John's dog has a pedigree, a record of its ancestors.
   record of its ancestors, context

2. George Gershwin composed, or wrote, that song.
   wrote, context

3. It was an uneventful drive until the storm hit.
   with no unusual event, word parts

4. We remade the guest room bed with clean sheets.
   made again, word parts

5. Ms. Lane loves biographies, which are true stories about the lives of real people.
   true stories about the lives of real people, context

6. Susie wrote her paper with care so it would be readable.
   able to be read, word parts

7. Oxygen is an example of an odorless gas.
   an odorless gas, context

8. Some words are unpronounceable.
   cannot be pronounced, word parts

9. The name for a turban, which is a soft hat with no brim, came from the Turkish language.
   soft hat with no brim, context

10. Deciduous trees—maples and oaks, for example—lose their leaves in winter.
    trees that lose their leaves in winter, context

Discovering New Words

Using Vocabulary in Writing

6

Here are four prefixes and four suffixes. Write two words that use each.
Answers will vary.

un _____   _____ er

un _____   _____ er

re _____   _____ able

re _____   _____ able

mis _____   _____ less

mis _____   _____ less

non _____   _____ ful

non _____   _____ ful

Now write four sentences. Use eight of the words above in your sentences.
Answers will vary.

_____

_____

_____

_____

_____

_____

_____

_____

_____

_____

_____

Skills Practice Book, Aqua Level
Copyright © by McDougal, Littell & Company

Review: Discovering New Words

Using Context Clues Each sentence below has a context clue in it. Draw two lines under the words that help explain the meaning of the underlined word.

1. The captain walked to the stern, the back, of the ship.
2. Tony rode on a monorail, which is a train that travels on one rail above the ground.
3. My grandmother knits sweaters, especially cardigans.
4. Dr. Stern is an oceanographer—a scientist who studies the ocean.
5. Amphibians, like frogs and toads, live almost everywhere on the earth.
6. The careless robber left a conspicuous, or obvious, trail.
7. Helen is allergic to dust. In other words, she is very sensitive to dust.
8. My mother cooks poultry, such as turkey or duck, for Thanksgiving.
9. The mountain looked gigantic, that is, very big.
10. Sailing ships, such as schooners, are slower than steamships.

Using Word Parts Answer these questions.

1. If *survive* means "to stay alive," what does *survivor* mean?

    someone who stays alive

2. If *fortunate* means "lucky," what does *unfortunate* mean?

    not lucky

3. If *guide* means "to lead," what does *misguide* mean?

    lead wrongly

4. If *worth* means "value," what does *worthless* mean?

    without value

5. If *notice* means "to see," what does *noticeable* mean?

    can be seen

6. If *construct* means "to build," what does *reconstruct* mean?

    to build again

What Is a Sentence?

Learning About Sentences

8

A sentence is a group of words that tells a complete thought. Each of these groups of words is a sentence.

Who or what?	What happened?
Alan	waxed the table.
The noisy clown	ran in circles.

Finding the Two Parts of a Sentence Read each sentence. Decide which words tell *who or what*. Decide which words tell *what happened.* Draw a line between the two parts of each sentence.

EXAMPLE: Lisa | ate a plum.

1. The phone | rang twice.
2. My aunt | owns a gift shop.
3. Turtles | move slowly.
4. The dentist | cleaned my teeth.
5. My best friend | lives next door.
6. Tracey | drew a colorful picture.
7. My lamb | won first prize at the fair.
8. Lawrence | played in the sandbox.
9. Trudy | mailed her letter.
10. Many ducks | swam in the pond.
11. Jeff | washed the fresh strawberries.
12. Hibiscus flowers | grow in Hawaii.
13. Rosa's father | visited friends in Mexico.
14. All the red balloons | popped.
15. Henry | spotted a tiny lizard.

Kinds of Sentences (1)

Learning About Sentences

There are four kinds of sentences. When you write sentences, you must show where each sentence begins and ends. Every sentence begins with a capital letter. Each kind of sentence uses a certain mark at the end. Here are two kinds.

A statement is a sentence that tells or states something. Use a period (**.**) at the end of every statement.

    The weather is hot.

A question is a sentence that asks something. Use a question mark (**?**) at the end of every question.

    Do you like hot weather?

Identifying Statements and Questions Write each sentence on the line. Use a capital letter at the beginning of each sentence and the correct mark at the end.

1. citrus fruits grow in Florida

   Citrus fruits grow in Florida.

2. do you like baked beans

   Do you like baked beans?

3. where will the airplane land

   Where will the airplane land?

4. we are going to visit a factory

   We are going to visit a factory.

5. when will the rain stop

   When will the rain stop?

6. my father jogs in the morning

   My father jogs in the morning.

7. people in Haiti speak French

   People in Haiti speak French.

8. did anyone water the plants

   Did anyone water the plants?

9. have you ever been in a canoe

   Have you ever been in a canoe?

10. the emu is a tall bird that cannot fly

    The emu is a tall bird that cannot fly.

Kinds of Sentences (2)

Learning About Sentences

10

You have already learned about two kinds of sentences, statements and questions. Here are two more kinds of sentences.

A command or request is a sentence that tells you to do something. Use a period (.) at the end of most commands and requests. Use an exclamation point (!) at the end of a command that shows strong feeling.

> Please set the table.   Look out!

An exclamation is a sentence that shows strong feeling. Use an exclamation point (!) at the end of every exclamation.

> The house is on fire!

Identifying Sentences Put the correct mark at the end of each sentence. Then tell whether it is a **statement, question, command,** or **exclamation.**

1. Please come on time**.**   **command**
2. Who ate the bagels**?**   **question**
3. How deep the snow is**!**   **exclamation**
4. Wait for me at the corner**.**   **command**
5. My sister has a cold**.**   **statement**
6. What a good time we had**!**   **exclamation**
7. How much does this record cost**?**   **question**
8. The children are in the park**.**   **statement**
9. Close the door**.**   **command**
10. What good players you are**!**   **exclamation**
11. How fast can you run**?**   **question**
12. Come home before dark**.**   **command**
13. Food gives your body energy**.**   **statement**
14. What time did the sun rise**?**   **question**
15. Watch out for that falling rock**!**   **exclamation**

Parts of the Sentence

Learning About Sentences

11

The **subject** of a sentence is the part that tells *whom or what* the sentence is about. It tells *who or what* does or is something. A subject may have one word or more than one word.

The subject of each of these sentences has a line under it.

<u>Thanksgiving</u> is my favorite holiday.
<u>All of the children</u> enjoyed the story.

The **predicate** of a sentence is the part that tells *what happened*. It tells about the subject. It can do one of these things:

Tell what the subject *does or did.*
Tell what the subject *is or was*

A predicate may have one word or more than one word. The predicate of each of these sentences has two lines under it.

Luke <u>coughed</u>. (What the subject *did*)
Nancy <u>is my friend</u>. (What the subject *is*)

Every sentence must have a subject and a predicate.

Finding Subjects and Predicates Draw one line under the subject of these sentences. Draw two lines under the predicate.

1. <u>Margie</u> <u>broke her leg</u>.
2. <u>My friends</u> <u>ride their bikes to the pool</u>.
3. <u>The Dallas Cowboys</u> <u>are my favorite players</u>.
4. <u>Mr. Evergates</u> <u>sells cars</u>.
5. <u>Many birds</u> <u>fly south for the winter</u>.
6. <u>Janet</u> <u>built a snowman</u>.
7. <u>Len's mother</u> <u>rides the bus to work</u>.
8. <u>A heavy fog</u> <u>hid the houses</u>.
9. <u>The soup</u> <u>was too hot</u>.
10. <u>Your clothes</u> <u>are dirty</u>.
11. <u>The fan</u> <u>cooled the room</u>.
12. <u>Darryl</u> <u>is a good singer</u>.
13. <u>A lion</u> <u>escaped from the zoo</u>!
14. <u>Sonya's family</u> <u>went to the beach</u>.
15. <u>The officer at the corner</u> <u>directed traffic</u>.

The Simple Subject

Learning About Sentences

12

When we divide a sentence into two parts, we call the subject part the **complete subject.** We call the predicate part the **complete predicate.**

The most important word in the complete subject is called the **simple subject.** If you leave out the simple subject, the sentence does not make sense. In the sentences below, the simple subject is underlined.

The <u>dog</u> barked.
The big <u>dog</u> barked.
My neighbor's big <u>dog</u> barked.

In a command, the subject is *you.* The word *you* is understood but not said.

(*You*) Sit over there.

Finding Simple Subjects Draw one line under the simple subject.

EXAMPLE: The large <u>spider</u> scared me.

1. The <u>pineapple</u> is sweet.
2. Don's <u>father</u> drives a delivery truck.
3. The <u>girls</u> played basketball.
4. <u>Betsy</u> raked the leaves in her grandmother's yard.
5. The noisy <u>crowd</u> cheered loudly.
6. Your <u>books</u> are on the table.
7. Strong <u>winds</u> blew down many branches.
8. Leslie's <u>sister</u> is a librarian.
9. Our <u>team</u> won the three-legged race.
10. The whole <u>band</u> marched in the parade.
11. The <u>clothes</u> in that store are expensive.
12. One <u>shelf</u> in the kitchen holds glasses.
13. Jon's <u>tadpole</u> slowly turned into a frog.
14. The <u>president</u> of the company works very hard.
15. My aunt's <u>children</u> are my cousins.

The Simple Predicate

Learning About Sentences

13

The most important word in the complete predicate is called the **simple predicate,** or the **verb.** Every sentence must have a verb. In the sentences below, each verb has two lines under it.

    The stars shone brightly in the sky.
    The stars shone brightly.
    The stars shone.

Most verbs show action. Other verbs say that something is. Some verbs of the second kind are these: *am, is, are, was,* and *were.*

Finding the Verb Draw two lines under the verb in each sentence below.

1. The baby crawled across the patio.
2. Thick fog is dangerous at sea.
3. Stories about ghosts sometimes frighten me.
4. The black horse jumped over the fence.
5. A loose branch fell against our house.
6. Members of the band sold tickets this afternoon.
7. That small striped kitten is eight weeks old.
8. The doctor bandaged my wrist.
9. The triplets' birthdays were in January.
10. A caterpillar ate the leaves of this plant.
11. Scientists from many countries studied Halley's comet.
12. One first grader was very upset.
13. Ten woolly sheep grazed in the meadow.
14. Scotland is next to England.
15. The Nile River flows through Egypt.

Mixed Practice: Learning About Sentences

Learning About Sentences 14

Identifying Parts of a Sentence Decide whether each group of words below is a sentence. If it is a sentence, write **sentence** on the line. If it is not a sentence, write **subject** after any word group that tells *who or what*. Write **predicate** after any word group that tells *what happened*.

1. My cousin Bill.   _subject_
2. Watered the tomato plants.   _predicate_
3. Maurice walked home.   _sentence_
4. Felt dizzy.   _predicate_
5. The new movie theater.   _subject_

Identifying the Four Kinds of Sentences Add the correct end mark to each sentence. Identify each by writing **statement**, **question**, **command**, or **exclamation** after the sentence.

1. Can you help me**?**   _question_
2. This is my friend, Rodrigo**.**   _statement_
3. How old is your turtle**?**   _question_
4. How fast you can run**!**   _exclamation_
5. Open this present first**.**   _command_

Finding Simple Subjects and Verbs Draw one line under the simple subject of the sentence and two lines under the simple predicate.

1. Sarah moved to Phoenix.
2. Jim's collection of baseball cards is valuable.
3. The ship crossed the Pacific Ocean.
4. The ranger in the park showed us the trail.
5. Raspberries grow wild behind our garage.

Using Sentences in Writing

Learning About Sentences
15

Has your class worked on a **class project** lately?
Do you have a **hobby?**
Has there been a **recent storm** that caused flooding or closed your school?
Have you learned a **new game** lately?
Do you have a pet? Do you have **problems with your pet?**
What is your **favorite book?**

Think about the questions above. Choose the one that is most interesting to you. Circle it. Then, on the lines below, write five questions about the subject you circled.

Trade papers with a classmate. Using another sheet of paper, answer the five questions your classmate wrote. You may use more than five sentences. Be sure to use capital letters and end marks correctly in both your questions and your answers.

When you are finished, trade your answers with your classmate.

_____
_____
_____
_____
_____
_____
_____
_____
_____
_____
_____
_____
_____
_____
_____

Review: Learning About Sentences

Making Sure That Sentences Are Complete If a word group tells *who or what* did something and *what happened,* write **Sentence.** If it does not, write **Not a sentence.**

1. Rang the doorbell.   <u>Not a sentence</u>

2. The statue in the park.   <u>Not a sentence</u>

3. Greg skates well.   <u>Sentence</u>

4. Three little kittens.   <u>Not a sentence</u>

5. Mr. Jackson painted his house.   <u>Sentence</u>

Identifying Sentences Write **statement, question, command,** or **exclamation** on the line next to each sentence. Put the correct mark at the end of every sentence.

1. Clean your room**.**   <u>command</u>

2. We had a picnic in the park**.**   <u>statement</u>

3. What a pretty flower that is**!**   <u>exclamation</u>

4. When is Memorial Day**?**   <u>question</u>

5. Please read this poem**.**   <u>command</u>

6. That car almost hit me**!**   <u>exclamation</u>

7. Snow fell last night**.**   <u>statement</u>

8. Did you enjoy the movie**?**   <u>question</u>

9. Listen carefully to the directions**.**   <u>command</u>

10. Why were the boys so late**?**   <u>question</u>

Finding Simple Subjects and Verbs Draw one line under the simple subject. Draw two lines under the verb.

1. Julio's <u>father</u> <u><u>is</u></u> a carpenter.

2. <u>Paula</u> <u><u>collected</u></u> seashells on the beach.

3. My <u>brother</u> <u><u>cut</u></u> his finger.

4. Terry's new <u>friend</u> <u><u>is</u></u> deaf.

5. The <u>mail</u> <u><u>arrived</u></u> late today.

What Are Nouns?

Understanding Nouns
17

Nouns are words that name persons, places, and things.
Here are some nouns:

NAMING PERSONS	NAMING PLACES	NAMING THINGS
Helen Keller	library	comb
brother	hospital	airplane
artist	Memphis	sandwich

The nouns above name things you can see. Some nouns name things you cannot see. Here are some nouns of this kind.

love   fear   kindness

Finding Nouns Draw a line under every noun in these sentences.

1. My <u>mother</u> drove to the <u>bank</u>.
2. <u>Curt</u> uses a <u>bookmark</u> in his <u>book</u>.
3. <u>London</u> is the <u>capital</u> of <u>England</u>.
4. The <u>wind</u> blew the <u>leaves</u> off the <u>trees</u>.
5. <u>Tom</u> and his <u>friends</u> painted the <u>fence</u>.
6. The <u>conductor</u> blew the <u>whistle</u> on the <u>train</u>.
7. <u>Connie</u> shoveled the <u>snow</u> off the <u>sidewalk</u>.
8. <u>Donna</u> heard a <u>noise</u> in the <u>attic</u>.
9. <u>Julie</u> is playing <u>tennis</u> at the <u>park</u>.
10. The <u>farmer</u> chased the <u>rabbit</u> out of his <u>garden</u>.
11. <u>Evelyn</u> showed <u>courage</u> during the <u>emergency</u>.
12. <u>Benito</u> has <u>talent</u> in <u>art</u>.

Using Nouns Name six things you wear.
Answers will vary.

_____   _____

_____   _____

_____   _____

Understanding Nouns

Using Nouns as Subjects

18

The simple subject is the word in a sentence that tells *whom or what* the sentence is about. Nouns are names of people, places, and things. They tell whom or what. Therefore, nouns may be used as simple subjects.

There are several nouns in this sentence:

> Larry set the plates on the table.

The noun that tells who or what did something is *Larry*. *Larry* is the simple subject of the sentence.

Finding Simple Subjects In each sentence, draw a line under the noun that is used as the simple subject.

1. <u>Amy</u> watered the flowers.
2. The young <u>skater</u> fell on the ice.
3. My <u>father</u> cooked hamburgers outside.
4. The <u>magician</u> performed many surprising tricks.
5. <u>Ostriches</u> cannot fly.
6. The <u>princess</u> wore a golden crown.
7. The <u>store</u> across the street opens at 9:00 A.M.
8. The <u>feathers</u> on that hat look silly.
9. Most <u>adults</u> can walk a mile in fifteen minutes.
10. The <u>tires</u> of this bike need more air.

Using Nouns as Subjects Each of these sentences needs a subject. In each blank, write a noun that can be used as the simple subject. **Answers will vary.**

1. _____ live in the desert.
2. _____ feel smooth.
3. _____ wear uniforms.
4. _____ are heavy.
5. _____ is sticky.

Common Nouns and Proper Nouns

Understanding Nouns
19

A common noun is a general name for persons, places, or things. A common noun begins with a small letter.

A proper noun names a particular person, place, or thing. A proper noun begins with a capital letter.

COMMON NOUNS	PROPER NOUNS
car	Mustang
monster	Godzilla
boy	Jack

A proper noun may be made up of more than one word. Capitalize all the important words in the proper noun. Do not capitalize *of, on,* or *the.*

Writing Proper Nouns After each of these common nouns, write the name of a particular person, place, or thing that the word makes you think of.
Nouns will vary.

1. teacher _____
2. girl _____
3. pet _____
4. cereal _____
5. store _____
6. movie _____
7. state _____
8. magazine _____
9. doctor _____
10. street _____

Finding Common Nouns and Proper Nouns Read each noun. If it is a common noun, write **C** on the short line. If it is a proper noun, write **P** on the line. Write every proper noun, beginning it with a capital letter.

EXAMPLE: snoopy __P__ *Snoopy*

1. carpet — C
2. radio — C
3. statue of liberty — P — **Statue of Liberty**
4. superman — P — **Superman**
5. refrigerator — C
6. grand canyon — P — **Grand Canyon**

Understanding Nouns
Singular Nouns and Plural Nouns
20

A **singular noun** names one person, place, or thing. A **plural noun** names more than one person, place, or thing.

Follow these rules for forming the plural of nouns.

1. **To form the plural of most nouns, add -s.**

    lamp<u>s</u>   fan<u>s</u>   block<u>s</u>   toy<u>s</u>

2. **When the singular form ends with s, sh, ch, or x, add -es.**

    glass<u>es</u>   bush<u>es</u>   coach<u>es</u>   fox<u>es</u>

3. **When the singular noun ends in a consonant and y, change the y to i and add -es.**

    fly—fl<u>ies</u>   blueberry—blueberr<u>ies</u>   daisy—dais<u>ies</u>

4. **For most nouns ending in f or fe, add -s. For some nouns ending in f or fe, change the f to v and add -es or -s.**

    dwarf—dwarf<u>s</u>   knife—kni<u>ves</u>   elf—el<u>ves</u>
    chief—chief<u>s</u>   wife—wi<u>ves</u>   leaf—lea<u>ves</u>

5. **Some nouns are the same for singular and plural.**

    moose   sheep   deer   fish

6. **Some nouns form their plurals in special ways.**

    child—children   man—men   woman—women
    foot—feet   goose—geese   tooth—teeth

Forming Plurals Write the plural form for each of these nouns.

1. woman _women_
2. horse _horses_
3. sky _skies_
4. cherry _cherries_
5. batch _batches_
6. nail _nails_
7. street _streets_
8. class _classes_
9. foot _feet_
10. baby _babies_

11. wife _wives_
12. ditch _ditches_
13. leaf _leaves_
14. deer _deer_
15. dish _dishes_
16. tooth _teeth_
17. toy _toys_
18. ax _axes_
19. chief _chiefs_
20. rash _rashes_

Making Nouns Show Possession

Understanding Nouns 21

A **possessive noun** is a noun that shows ownership. It tells whom or what the noun following it belongs to. *Fran's coat* means the coat that belongs to Fran. *Fran's* is a possessive noun.

Follow these rules for making nouns show possession.

To make a singular noun show ownership, add an apostrophe and *s*.

doctor—doctor**'s**   Kristen—Kristen**'s**

There are two rules for making plural nouns show ownership.

If the plural noun ends in *s*, simply add an apostrophe after the *s*.

swimmers—swimmers**'**   judges—judges**'**

If the plural noun does not end in *s*, add an apostrophe and an *s* after the apostrophe.

children—children**'s**   women—women**'s**

If you are not sure where to add the apostrophe, write the word by itself. Then follow the above rules. When you write 's in cursive handwriting, do not connect the *s* to the last letter of the word. The apostrophe should separate the two letters.

Writing Possessive Forms of Nouns
Make these nouns show possession. Write the word first. Then add the apostrophe, or apostrophe and *s*.

1. hiker — **hiker's**
2. Bess — **Bess's**
3. brother — **brother's**
4. speaker — **speaker's**
5. fish — **fish's**
6. snowmen — **snowmen's**
7. members — **members'**
8. babies — **babies'**
9. deer — **deer's**
10. friends — **friends'**

Using Possessives
Make each underlined noun show possession.

1. The <u>men</u> coats are in the closet.   **men's**
2. <u>Emilio</u> family is on vacation.   **Emilio's**
3. My <u>kitten</u> fur is striped.   **kitten's**
4. The <u>animals</u> cages must be locked.   **animals'**
5. I listened to my <u>mother</u> records.   **mother's**

Mixed Practice: Understanding Nouns

Finding and Writing Nouns Draw a line under each noun in these sentences. Circle each proper noun that should begin with a capital letter. Then draw a second line under the noun that is the simple subject of the sentence.

1. My favorite <u>aunt</u> lives in (houston), (texas).
2. Our <u>class</u> visited the (milwaukee) (zoo).
3. (Jean) wrote a report about camels.
4. The baby <u>elephant</u> with big ears was called (dumbo).
5. The <u>audience</u> at the circus laughed at the clowns.
6. The <u>class</u> memorized the (declaration) of (independence).
7. (Coretta) cooked chicken for dinner on (sunday).
8. (Mario) works in the lab on (wednesdays).
9. The <u>baby</u> in the stroller clapped his hands and smiled.
10. The <u>cheerleaders</u> practiced before the game.

Making Nouns Show Possession After each sentence, write **S** if the underlined word is singular; write **P** if it is plural. Then make the underlined words show possession.

1. The children laughed at the <u>monkey</u> tricks. __S__ __monkey's__
2. The <u>dogs</u> water dishes are empty. __P__ __dogs'__
3. The <u>ship</u> crew repaired the sails. __S__ __ship's__
4. Our <u>neighbors</u> yard is full of flowers. __P__ __neighbors'__
5. <u>Elana</u> poems will be printed in our school paper. __S__ __Elana's__
6. Did you see the <u>birds</u> nest? __P__ __birds'__
7. Two <u>schools</u> bands marched in the parade. __P__ __schools'__
8. <u>Gary</u> mother drove us to the theater. __S__ __Gary's__
9. <u>Grandfather</u> wood carvings are spectacular. __S__ __Grandfather's__
10. The <u>painter</u> ladder is too short to reach the roof. __S__ __painter's__

Using Nouns in Writing

Understanding Nouns
23

You have learned that there are five kinds of nouns.

1. Common nouns are general names for persons, places, and things. Write three common nouns.
Nouns throughout will vary.

_____ _____ _____

2. Proper nouns name a particular person, place, or thing. Write three proper nouns.

_____ _____ _____

3. Singular nouns name one person, place, or thing. Write three singular nouns.

_____ _____ _____

4. Plural nouns name more than one person, place, or thing. Write three plural nouns.

_____ _____ _____

5. Possessive nouns show ownership. Write three possessive nouns.

_____ _____ _____

Now write five sentences. Use at least two nouns in each sentence. In the first sentence, there must be at least one common noun. The second sentence must use at least one proper noun. Use a singular noun in the third sentence and a plural noun in the fourth. The last sentence should use a possessive noun.
Sentences will vary.

_____

_____

_____

_____

_____

_____

_____

_____

Review: Understanding Nouns

Finding Simple Subjects Draw two lines under the noun that is used as the simple subject in each sentence. Underline all the other nouns once.

1. <u><u>Cinderella</u></u> lost her shiny <u>slipper</u>.
2. The <u>band</u> played my favorite <u>song</u>.
3. Our <u><u>team</u></u> won the <u>game</u>.
4. The crying <u><u>baby</u></u> on the <u>bus</u> was hungry.
5. My <u><u>grandfather</u></u> was born in <u>Europe</u>.

Finding Common Nouns and Proper Nouns Find the proper nouns in this list. Write each proper noun correctly on the lines below.

fence　　　monday　　　airport　　　montana
senator glenn　　the liberty bell　　ohio river　　museum

Senator Glenn　　　　　　　　　　Ohio River

Monday　　　　　　　　　　　　　Montana

the Liberty Bell

Forming Plurals Write the plural form for each of these nouns.

1. number — numbers
2. puppy — puppies
3. dress — dresses
4. shelf — shelves
5. foot — feet
6. child — children
7. sheep — sheep
8. tax — taxes
9. boot — boots
10. brush — brushes

Making Nouns Show Possession Write the possessive forms of these nouns.

1. Charles — Charles's
2. geese — geese's
3. winners — winners'
4. women — women's
5. camel — camel's
6. uncle — uncle's
7. sharks — sharks'
8. shoppers — shoppers'
9. captain — captain's
10. states — states'

What Are Verbs?

Understanding Verbs
25

Words that tell about action are called **verbs**. Many verbs tell about actions you can see.

    Tracey <u>jumped</u> rope.   The ball <u>bounced</u> down the steps.

Other verbs tell about actions you cannot see.

    Laura <u>wished</u> on a star.   Earl <u>dislikes</u> radishes.

Finding Action Verbs Underline the action verb in each sentence.

1. Mark <u>slid</u> on the ice.
2. Janice <u>climbed</u> the steep hill.
3. The hot children <u>dove</u> into the pool.
4. All the sherbet quickly <u>melted</u>.
5. Elizabeth <u>wants</u> ballet slippers.
6. The butterfly <u>landed</u> on the daisy.
7. The chef <u>added</u> scallions to the salad.
8. Siamese cats <u>have</u> blue eyes.
9. Ramona <u>traveled</u> to Arizona.
10. Our dog <u>chews</u> holes in the rug.

Using Action Verbs Fill in the blanks with action verbs that will complete each sentence. **Verbs will vary.**

1. The young horse _____ across the field.
2. Joyce _____ a letter.
3. Our fourth-grade class _____ the zoo.
4. Ernie _____ a sandwich.
5. The talented artist _____ a picture.
6. I _____ the papers.
7. Brian _____ his hair.
8. The girls _____ to school.

Verbs That Tell That Something Is

Understanding Verbs
26

Some verbs do not tell about action. These verbs say that something is. Here are some examples:

I <u>am</u> happy.   Mrs. Evans <u>is</u> our bus driver.

Here are some verbs that say that something is:

am   is   are   was   were

Finding the Verb Underline the verb in each sentence.

1. I <u>am</u> busy.
2. The scarecrow <u>is</u> in the cornfield.
3. You <u>were</u> the star of the show.
4. Edward <u>was</u> in his room.
5. Mexico and Canada <u>are</u> our neighbors.
6. I <u>am</u> hungry.
7. That plum <u>was</u> sweet.
8. The flowers <u>were</u> in the new vase.

Finding Two Kinds of Verbs Underline the verb in each sentence. Write **A** if it is an action verb, and **I** if it says that something is.

__I__	1. Dina <u>is</u> our club's treasurer.
__A__	2. The dog <u>chased</u> the stick.
__I__	3. Redwoods <u>are</u> very tall trees.
__A__	4. Erin <u>plays</u> the piano beautifully.
__I__	5. Abraham Lincoln <u>was</u> an honest man.
__I__	6. Jason <u>is</u> in my music class.
__A__	7. Bears usually <u>like</u> honey.
__I__	8. Those puzzles <u>were</u> hard.
__A__	9. The police officer <u>blew</u> her whistle.
__A__	10. Alan <u>wrote</u> a poem.

Main Verbs and Helping Verbs

Understanding Verbs 27

A verb may be a single word or a group of words. A verb with more than one word is made up of a *main verb* and one or more *helping verbs*. The last word is the **main verb.** The parts of the verb that come before the main verb are the **helping verbs.** Here are some examples.

	HELPING VERBS	MAIN VERB
The baby is crying.	is	crying
The flowers should have bloomed.	should have	bloomed

The main verb often ends in *-ing* or *-ed*.
Here are some verbs that are often used as helping verbs.

am	have	do	shall
is	has	does	should
are	had	did	may
was	can	will	might
were	could	would	

Finding Main Verbs and Helping Verbs Underline the main verb in each sentence once. Underline the helping verbs twice.

EXAMPLE: I have finished my work.

1. My mother might come to our play.
2. Curtis has dried the dishes.
3. I should have brought an umbrella.
4. Audrey will play the violin for us.
5. You may take another piece of cake.
6. The girls have learned a new stunt.
7. The horses were racing to the finish line.
8. Strong winds have blown the papers all over.
9. Billy can skate well.
10. Miguel does study hard.
11. Martha was weeding the garden.
12. The Bensons are moving to a new apartment.
13. One acrobat is performing now.
14. The twins have slept all afternoon.
15. We could wash the windows today.

Using Helping Verbs

Understanding Verbs
28

Follow these rules for using helping verbs.

Always use helping verbs with these four verbs:

    been   done   seen   gone

Verbs that end in *-en* must be used with helping verbs.

    Jeff *has chosen* his prize.   We *have given* our promise.

Verbs that end in *-ing* must be used with helping verbs.

    You *were singing* loud.   Tam *is being* a good dog.

Using Helping Verbs Read each sentence. If it is correct, write **Correct** on the line. If the verb needs a helping verb, write a helping verb and the main verb.

    EXAMPLE: __has seen__ Kerry seen that movie.

__is *or* was watching__ 1. Lou watching the football game.

__has *or* had broken__ 2. Marita broken her glasses.

__Correct__ 3. Beverly has gone to Missouri.

__is *or* was swinging__ 4. The monkey swinging from the tree.

__has *or* had been saving__ 5. Shawn been saving his money.

__has *or* had eaten__ 6. Samantha eaten an avocado.

__Correct__ 7. We might be going to the circus.

__is *or* was ringing__ 8. The phone ringing.

__Correct__ 9. Dennis will be visiting his grandfather.

__Correct__ 10. The pioneers were building a cabin.

__has *or* had done__ 11. Ed done his work.

__Correct__ 12. Maureen had written her report.

__have *or* had seen__ 13. I seen a giant footprint.

__is *or* was playing__ 14. The orchestra playing a waltz.

__Correct__ 15. This crab is walking backwards.

Separated Parts of Verbs

Understanding Verbs
29

The helping verbs and main verb are sometimes separated by other words that are not verbs. Here are some examples.

>Amanda **has** never **been** late.
>We **could** not **hear** the directions.
>Dan **does**n't **like** hot weather.

Notice that *not* and *n't* are not verbs.

Questions often begin with a helping verb. Other parts of the sentence come between the helping verb and the main verb.

>**Have** you **read** this book?

Finding Separated Parts of the Verb Underline the main verb in each sentence once. Underline the helping verbs twice.

EXAMPLE: <u><u>Did</u></u> you <u>hear</u> the thunder?

1. Amy <u><u>had</u></u> never <u>visited</u> Israel before.
2. Benjamin <u><u>wouldn't</u></u> <u>tell</u> anyone our secret.
3. Lorenzo <u><u>has</u></u> often <u>been</u> helpful.
4. The scientist <u><u>could</u></u> not <u>remember</u> the formula.
5. <u><u>May</u></u> Kate <u>play</u> outside?
6. I <u><u>have</u></u> never <u>met</u> your younger brother.
7. <u><u>Does</u></u> this model airplane <u>cost</u> much?
8. The queen <u><u>has</u></u> just <u>arrived</u>.
9. You <u><u>should</u></u> not <u>pick</u> the flowers.
10. JoAnne <u><u>has</u></u> always <u>been</u> a fast runner.
11. Mr. Carney <u><u>is</u></u> usually <u>working</u> in his garden.
12. Lamont <u><u>has</u></u> never <u>had</u> the chicken pox.
13. <u><u>Was</u></u> Carol <u>fixing</u> the peanut butter sandwiches?
14. The baby <u><u>can't</u></u> <u>walk</u> yet.
15. Why <u><u>did</u></u> Jack <u>jump</u> over the candlestick?

Understanding Verbs

Using the Right Form of *Be*

30

These are the forms of the verb *be*:

am	was	be
is	were	being
are		been

Be sure to follow these five rules when using the forms of the verb *be*.

1. Use a helping verb before the forms *be*, *being*, and *been*. Do not use one of these forms alone or as the only helping verb before a main verb.

   I *will be* late.   You *were being helped*.   We *have been* cold.

2. If the subject names one person, place, or thing, use the form *is* or *was*.

   Andrea *is* here.   Vincent *was* at school.

3. If the subject names more than one person, place, or thing, use the form *are* or *were*.

   The girls *are* here.   The boys *were* at school.

4. When the subject is *you*, use the form *are* or *were*.

   You *are* correct.   You *were studying* hard.

5. When the subject is *I*, use the form *am* or *was*.

   I *am* correct.   I *was studying* hard.

Using the Right Form of *Be* Underline the correct form of the verb *be*.

1. I (been, <u>was</u>) waiting for the bus.
2. You (<u>are</u>, is) going the wrong way.
3. Mandy (<u>was</u>, were) standing in line.
4. The spider (<u>was</u>, been) spinning a web.
5. The girls (<u>are</u>, is) blowing up balloons.
6. Frank (been, <u>is</u>) looking for his dog.
7. My brother (be, <u>is</u>) mowing the lawn.
8. The police officer (<u>was</u>, were) directing traffic.
9. The band members (was, <u>were</u>) marching in the parade.
10. You (been, <u>have been</u>) elected class secretary.
11. I (<u>am</u>, is) excited about the baseball game.
12. Diane (<u>is</u>, being) my best friend.

Using Contractions

Understanding Verbs
31

Sometimes a verb is combined with another word to make a new word. This new word is called a **contraction.** When a contraction is made, at least one letter is dropped. We use an **apostrophe (')** to show where letters are left out. For example, *is not* becomes *isn't*. The "o" in *not* is dropped, and an apostrophe takes its place.

Here are some contractions we use often.

I am	I'm	are not	aren't
I will	I'll	was not	wasn't
I had	I'd	do not	don't
he would	he'd	did not	didn't
she is	she's	have not	haven't
she has	she's	can not	can't
it is	it's	will not	won't
it has	it's	could not	couldn't
you are	you're	here is	here's
they have	they've	where is	where's

Making Contractions Make contractions from these pairs of words.

1. have not   **haven't**
2. they would   **they'd**
3. was not   **wasn't**
4. I will   **I'll**
5. he has   **he's**
6. there is   **there's**
7. do not   **don't**
8. it is   **it's**
9. will not   **won't**
10. she would   **she'd**
11. could not   **couldn't**
12. you have   **you've**

Identifying Contractions After each contraction, write the two words it is made from.

1. you're   **you are**
2. won't   **will not**
3. here's   **here is**
4. didn't   **did not**
5. I've   **I have**
6. he'll   **he will**
7. haven't   **have not**
8. they've   **they have**
9. can't   **can not**
10. aren't   **are not**

Using Negatives Correctly

Understanding Verbs
32

The words *no* and *not* are called **negatives.**

Some contractions are made by joining *not* with certain verbs, like this: *was* + *not* = *wasn't*. Words made in this way are also negatives.

The following words mean *no* or have *no* in them. Like *no* and *not,* they are negatives.

no	nobody	none	never
no one	nothing	nowhere	

Two negatives used together are called a **double negative.** Do not use double negatives.

WRONG: Daryl won't go nowhere.
RIGHT: Daryl won't go anywhere. *or* Daryl will go nowhere.

Using Negatives Correctly Underline the correct word.

1. Matt hadn't done (**any**, no) work.
2. Lydia didn't see (no one, **anyone**) in the park.
3. That store isn't (never, **ever**) open on Sundays.
4. I don't know (**anyone**, no one) in St. Louis.
5. Joyce (hasn't, **has**) no school supplies.
6. Heather couldn't find (**anything**, nothing) that fit her.
7. There isn't (nobody, **anybody**) at the ticket office.
8. Lea hasn't heard (**any**, none) of our songs.
9. Raul (**could**, couldn't) eat no more grapes.
10. Hal won't go (**anywhere**, nowhere) without his lucky penny.
11. Olivia has (any, **no**) more pencils. May she use one of yours?
12. Won't (nobody, **anybody**) help us?
13. I really don't want (**any**, no) more snacks.
14. There isn't (**anything**, nothing) left of the lost colony.
15. Tom won't (**ever**, never) ride a motorcycle.

Mixed Practice (1): Understanding Verbs

Understanding Verbs 33

Finding Verbs Underline every verb in each sentence. Underline both helping verbs and main verbs.

1. Erin <u>studied</u> the chart.
2. <u>Did</u> Leif Ericsson <u>discover</u> America first?
3. Raisins <u>are</u> naturally sweet.
4. The kittens <u>were</u> <u>purring</u> softly.
5. The whale <u>is</u> not a fish.
6. Your ideas <u>were</u> helpful.
7. Scientists <u>have</u> never <u>found</u> a cure for colds.
8. The robot <u>was</u> <u>signaling</u> a message.
9. Myles <u>pushed</u> the broom.
10. The gerbil <u>ran</u> through the maze.
11. Two buses <u>should</u> <u>arrive</u> this afternoon.
12. The Erie Canal <u>was</u> <u>completed</u> in 1825.
13. Todd and Karen <u>are</u> neighbors.
14. The library <u>closes</u> at eight o'clock.
15. Our team <u>has</u> <u>been</u> <u>winning</u> every game.

Using the Right Form of *Be* Underline the correct form in each sentence.

1. Chris and Sheri (<u>were</u>, was) roller skating.
2. (<u>Are</u>, Is) you boys using the jigsaw?
3. The sky (were, <u>was</u>) growing dark and cloudy.
4. Mike (<u>is</u>, be) my tennis partner.
5. We (<u>were</u>, been) looking for you.
6. One musician (<u>was</u>, were) playing a lute.
7. Real pandas (is, <u>are</u>) found in China.
8. I (be, <u>am</u>) getting a basket for my bike.
9. (Were, <u>Was</u>) Elise going to the Science Fair?
10. They (be, <u>will be</u>) coming here before long.

Mixed Practice (2): Understanding Verbs

Using Contractions Write the contraction for the underlined words.

1. I would love to visit China. __**I'd**__
2. We have not named the hamster. __**haven't**__
3. Judy would not ride the roller coaster. __**wouldn't**__
4. You are taller than Kara. __**You're**__
5. She will read us a story. __**She'll**__
6. This is not my scarf. __**isn't**__
7. Carl will not need a cast on his leg. __**won't**__
8. Brenda should not have cooked so much rice. __**shouldn't**__
9. Sandy does not need any more paper. __**doesn't**__
10. Did not you ride your bicycle? __**Didn't**__

Using Negatives Correctly Underline the correct word in the parentheses. Then underline each verb twice.

1. Susan can't (ever, never) stay up late.
2. Brad didn't go (nowhere, anywhere) without his watch.
3. Can't (anyone, no one) join your club?
4. Rosa (won't, will) never hurt animals.
5. My dog shouldn't grow (any, no) bigger.
6. Nobody (never, ever) uses that road.
7. I haven't found (nobody, anybody) at home.
8. There (wasn't, was) no cake left on the plate.
9. This book doesn't tell (nothing, anything) about Eskimos.
10. The boys did not find (any, no) buried treasure.

Using Verbs in Writing

Understanding Verbs
35

● Think about a person who is special to you. Answer these questions about him or her.

1. What is the person's name? _____

2. Where did you meet? _____

3. How long have you known each other? _____

4. What do you like best about the person? _____

5. What times have you had fun together? _____

6. What nice things has this person done for you? _____

Write a paragraph about this person. Try to use as many of the answers above as you can in your paragraph.

●
_____
_____
_____
_____
_____
_____
_____
_____
_____
_____
_____

● Look back at the sentences in your paragraph. Underline every verb. Decide which verbs are helping verbs. Write **HV** above each one. Find all of the contractions in your paragraph. Write **C** above each one.

Review: Understanding Verbs

Finding Two Kinds of Verbs Underline the verb in each sentence. Write **A** if it is an action verb, and **I** if it says that something is.

__I__ 1. A pointer <u>is</u> a hunting dog.

__A__ 2. The lights <u>blinked</u> a warning.

__A__ 3. Mr. Revere <u>carved</u> pictures in the wood.

__A__ 4. Tom <u>knew</u> the correct answer.

__A__ 5. The agent <u>decoded</u> the secret message.

Finding Main Verbs and Helping Verbs Underline the main verb once and the helping verbs twice.

1. Steve's mother <u>was</u> <u>jogging</u> in the park.
2. Maya <u>has</u> <u>taken</u> our picture.
3. A dentist <u>will be</u> <u>speaking</u> to our class.
4. You girls <u>might</u> <u>win</u> the championship.
5. An optician <u>should have</u> <u>checked</u> your eyes.
6. Lightning <u>did</u> not <u>strike</u> our house.
7. The spaceship <u>has</u> just <u>landed</u> in the desert.
8. <u>Have</u> you ever <u>climbed</u> that tree?
9. I <u>will</u> <u>catch</u> a huge fish.
10. Miguel <u>is</u> <u>wearing</u> a sombrero.

Using Contractions Make contractions from these pairs of words.

1. is not   __isn't__
2. was not   __wasn't__
3. where is   __where's__
4. you are   __you're__
5. does not   __doesn't__

6. he would   __he'd__
7. it is   __it's__
8. have not   __haven't__
9. will not   __won't__
10. I will   __I'll__

Avoiding Sentence Fragments

Writing Better Sentences
37

A sentence must tell a complete thought. Each sentence has two parts. One part, the subject, tells whom or what the sentence is about. The other part, the predicate, tells what the subject does or is.

If a group of words is missing one of these two parts, it is not a sentence. It is a **fragment,** or part of a sentence. Read these groups of words.

  The runner at first base.   Slid into second.

Both word groups are fragments. The first group does not tell what the runner did. It is missing a predicate. The second group does not tell who slid into second. It is missing a subject.

You can change a fragment into a sentence in two ways:

1. You can add words to complete the sentence.

The runner at first base took off.

2. You can combine a fragment with another sentence.

The runner at first base took off and slid into second.

Avoiding Sentence Fragments Decide whether each word group below is a sentence or a fragment. If it is a sentence, write **Sentence.** If it is a fragment, rewrite it and add words to make it a sentence.

Rewritten sentences will vary.

1. Called my mother. _____**(fragment)**_____

2. The grandfather clock. _____**(fragment)**_____

3. Helen returned her library book. _____**Sentence**_____

4. Robins' eggs are blue. _____**Sentence**_____

5. Frank read the newspaper. _____**Sentence**_____

6. The fourth grade. _____**(fragment)**_____

7. Chased the butterflies with a net. _____**(fragment)**_____

8. Martin forgot his lunch. _____**Sentence**_____

9. The ice melted. _____**Sentence**_____

10. The speeding car. _____**(fragment)**_____

Avoiding Run-on Sentences

Writing Better Sentences
38

A **run-on sentence** contains two or more complete thoughts that are not connected. These thoughts should be written as separate sentences.

This is a run-on sentence:

Ann has a new camera she takes many pictures.

It should be written like this:

Ann has a new camera. She takes many pictures.

When you separate the thoughts in a run-on sentence, remember to begin each new sentence with a capital letter. Put a period, question mark, or exclamation point at the end of each sentence.

Keeping Thoughts Apart Some of the following groups of words are correct sentences. Others are run-ons. If the word group is a run-on, decide where the first thought ends. Draw a line between the two thoughts. If the word group is a sentence, write **S** in the blank.

   EXAMPLE: Ross likes dogs | he owns a collie.

_____   1. Jon ran up the hill | he is tired.

_____   2. It's a beautiful day | the sun is shining.

_____   3. Tomorrow is Carla's birthday | she is having a party.

__S____   4. Valerie rides her bike to school every day.

__S____   5. Raymond visited a horse farm in Kentucky.

_____   6. That building is tall | it has thirty stories.

__S____   7. The turtle crawled slowly across the rocks.

_____   8. This syrup came from Vermont | it is maple syrup.

__S____   9. We went to a pancake breakfast at our school.

_____   10. The two homes look alike | they are both white.

Writing Compound Sentences

Writing Better Sentences
39

- Sometimes you may put two complete thoughts in one sentence, called a **compound sentence.** Follow these guidelines to write a compound sentence.

  1. The two thoughts must be about the same topic. These two sentences could be combined:

  I will bring sandwiches. You can bring juice.

These two sentences should not be combined:

  We are planning a picnic. I like to play soccer.

  2. Use a comma and one of these words to connect the two thoughts: *and, or, but.* Read these examples:

  I will bring sandwiches, and you can bring juice.
  We will go to the movie, or we will stay home.
  My family planned a picnic, but it rained.

  3. Do not combine more than two thoughts in one sentence. A sentence with three or more complete thoughts is called a **stringy sentence.** A stringy sentence should be broken into at least two sentences.

  Stringy: A bluejay landed in our yard and my cat chased it and it flew away.
  Corrected: A bluejay landed in our yard. My cat chased it, and it flew away.

- **Writing Compound Sentences** Combine each pair of sentences into a compound sentence. Use correct punctuation and combining words.

  1. Mom washed the dishes. I dried them.

     Mom washed the dishes, and I dried them.

  2. Do you like apricots? Do you prefer peaches?

     Do you like apricots, or do you prefer peaches?

  3. Hilary went shopping. She didn't buy anything.

     Hilary went shopping, but she didn't buy anything.

  4. Joel worked on the lamp. He fixed it.

     Joel worked on the lamp, and he fixed it.

  5. The Smiths have a big yard. They never use it.

     The Smiths have a big yard, but they never use it.

- **Combining Thoughts Correctly** Rewrite this stringy sentence as three sentences.
  Sentences may vary slightly. A possible answer is given.
  Dan was my friend and he moved away but I have not forgotten him
  and I will write a letter to him. **Dan was my friend. He moved away, but I have not forgotten him. I will write a letter to him.**

Using Sentences in Writing

Suppose you lived in an underground city.

    How would you travel to places in the city?

    What would your home be like?

    What would your school be like?

    How else would your life be different?

Write several sentences about living in an underground city. At least one sentence must be a compound sentence. It must tell two thoughts. Follow these guides for writing compound sentences.

1. The two thoughts must be about the same topic.
2. Use a comma and one of these words to connect the two thoughts: *and, but, or*.
3. Do not combine more than two thoughts in one sentence.

_____

_____

_____

_____

_____

_____

_____

_____

_____

_____

_____

_____

_____

Review: Writing Better Sentences

Identifying Fragments, Run-ons, and Correct Sentences Some of the following groups of words are correct sentences. Some are fragments. Others are run-ons. If the word group is a correct sentence, write **S** on the line. If the group is a fragment, write **F**. If the group is a run-on, write **R**.

_**R**_ 1. George walked to the library he returned some books.

_**S**_ 2. Dorrie hung her new raincoat in the closet.

_**F**_ 3. Hortense an unusual name.

_**R**_ 4. This is good bread may I have another slice?

_**R**_ 5. Debby plays on a softball team she is the pitcher.

_**R**_ 6. Luis is hungry he needs a sandwich.

_**F**_ 7. The worst apple in the barrel.

_**S**_ 8. The farmer plants his crops in the spring.

_**R**_ 9. That game was fun let's play it again.

_**F**_ 10. Felt funny and went home.

_**S**_ 11. Our cat sleeps on the windowsill.

_**R**_ 12. Melissa has new skates they are red.

_**F**_ 13. An angry tiger through the forest.

_**S**_ 14. The robin built a nest in the maple tree.

_**F**_ 15. Usually feeds the animals in the evening.

Combining Thoughts Correctly The following word group has several ideas strung together with *and*'s. Rewrite the stringy sentence as three sentences.
Sentences may vary slightly. A possible answer is given.
Jason visited a farm and he saw many animals and he fed the chickens and he collected their eggs.

**Jason visited a farm. He saw many animals. He fed the chickens, and he collected their eggs.**

What Is a Paragraph?

Writing a Paragraph
42

A paragraph is a group of sentences about one main idea. Here is an example of a paragraph.

> Hawaii is a special state. In 1959, it was the last of the fifty states to become part of the United States. It is the only state that is made entirely of islands. One hundred thirty-two islands make up the state of Hawaii. Hawaii is the only state that is not on the continent of North America. It lies in the Pacific Ocean.

The paragraph has six sentences. The first line of the paragraph is indented. That means it begins a few spaces to the right of the margin. The paragraph is about one main idea. The main idea is *why the state of Hawaii is special.*

Studying Paragraphs Read each paragraph. Then answer the questions.

> Learn to protect yourself from lightning when you are outside. During a thunderstorm, do not stand under a tall tree. Stay away from lakes and pools. Avoid touching metal objects. If you are in an open area, sit down and crouch. Most important, look for shelter. Get inside a building or a car.

1. How many sentences does this paragraph have? __7__

2. What is the main idea? __how to protect yourself from lightning__

> Stamp collecting is a hobby that will introduce you to a whole new world. You can discover strange animals or beautiful works of art on stamps. You can meet famous people. With stamps you can even travel to distant lands.

1. How many sentences does this paragraph have? __4__

2. What is the main idea? __how stamp collecting introduces a new world__

> The old bicycle needed repair. Its handlebar was loose. Its seat was frayed and worn. The blue paint on the frame was scratched and faded. Both tires were flat. No one could ride it in its present state.

1. How many sentences does this paragraph have? __6__

2. What is the main idea? __why the bicycle needed repair__

The Topic Sentence

The topic sentence gives the main idea of the paragraph. It tells what the whole paragraph is about. It is often the first sentence in the paragraph.

Read the following paragraph. The topic sentence is underlined.

<u>Mexico owes much to its Indian background.</u> Some Mexican foods are Indian. One well-known food is the tortilla—a kind of thin pancake made of cornmeal. Indians were making tortillas long before the Spanish arrived. The faces of most Mexicans look more Indian than Spanish. Even the name of the country is Indian. It is named for the Aztec god of war, Mexitili.

The topic sentence tells you that the paragraph is about Mexico's Indian background. The rest of the sentences add to, or develop, the main idea. The other sentences are about Indian foods, Indian faces, and an Indian name.

Studying Topic Sentences Read each paragraph below. Find and underline the topic sentence of each one.

1. <u>Tad enjoyed staying in a motel on his vacation.</u> It was much more exciting than being at home. The bed seemed comfortable. Tad could see the TV from anywhere in the room. The motel had a swimming pool, and Tad swam every morning and every evening. Best of all, he got to stay up much later than when he was at home.

2. <u>It is easy to make a paper bag mask.</u> You need only a paper bag, scissors, crayons, colored paper, and glue. Draw a face on the bag and cut holes for your eyes, nose, and mouth. Cut strips of colored paper for hair or a beard. Paste them on the bag. Put the bag on your head and have a good time!

Choosing a Topic Sentence This paragraph is missing a topic sentence. Three sentences are listed below it. Underline the sentence that would make the best topic sentence.

_____ I love the smell of turkey and pumpkin pie. I enjoy seeing my whole family come together for a delicious Thanksgiving dinner. I look forward to breaking the wishbone with my younger sister.

1. Thanksgiving is the last Thursday of November.
2. We remember the story of the first Thanksgiving.
3. <u>Thanksgiving is my favorite holiday.</u>

The Sentences in a Paragraph

Writing a Paragraph 44

The topic sentence tells the main idea of the paragraph. All the other sentences in the paragraph should tell more about, or develop, the main idea. Any sentence that does not tell about the main idea should not be included in the paragraph.

Read this paragraph. Find the topic sentence. Decide which sentence does not tell about the main idea.

> The peanut has many uses. People eat roasted peanuts and peanut butter. Peanut oil is used to oil machinery. The oil is also used in soap, face powder, shampoo, paint, and even explosives. The state of Georgia grows many peanuts. Peanut shells are used in plastics, wall board, and fertilizer.

The topic sentence tells you that the paragraph is about the many uses of the peanut. All but one of the other sentences tell uses for parts of the peanut. The sentence about Georgia does not tell about the uses of the peanut. It does not belong in the paragraph.

Studying Sentences in a Paragraph Read each paragraph below. Underline the topic sentence in each. Circle the sentence that does not belong.

1. <u>Certain signs may tell you when a person has not had enough sleep.</u> The person can become short-tempered and have little energy. He or she might make mistakes. The person may not be able to pay attention for long. He or she may doze off for short periods of time. (Some people sleep on mattresses that are too soft.)

2. <u>Making a house of playing cards takes patience.</u> First, you stand up two cards on their sides. Let the middle of one card rest against the end of the other card. (Solitaire is a card game you play by yourself.) The cards will hold each other up. Then you can add more cards at the open ends.

3. <u>Jamie's first ride on a horse was scary.</u> She put her foot in the groom's hand. As he boosted her up onto the saddle, she almost fell off the other side of the horse. Finally, she got her feet in the stirrups. She felt like she was a hundred feet off the ground! (The saddle was trimmed in silver.) She grabbed the horn of the saddle tightly as the horse took some steps. Jamie was sure she would fall and break every bone in her body.

Prewriting: Planning a Paragraph

Writing a Paragraph 45

You can use a process, or set of steps, for writing a paragraph. These steps include prewriting, writing a draft, revising and proofreading, and making and sharing a final copy.

Prewriting is the thinking and planning you do before you write. To plan your paragraph, follow these prewriting steps.

1. Make a list of all possible topics you could write about. Choose the topic that gives you the most ideas and is the most interesting.
2. Write several ideas, or notes, about your topic. Each note can be short phrases or even single words.
3. Read over your notes. Notice which ones fit together and tell about one idea. This idea will be the main idea of your paragraph. Write this idea at the bottom of your list.
4. Read your list of notes again. Cross out the ideas that do not fit together with the main idea. Add any new ideas you think of.

Here is how one girl, Becky, planned her paragraph. First, she made a list of topics. She chose to write about her school carnival. These are the notes she wrote:

parents volunteer win a goldfish
many games and prizes Treasure Chest
haunted house PTA runs it

Becky read over her notes and decided her main idea would be "things you can do at the carnival." She read her list of notes and crossed out "parents volunteer." It did not fit with her main idea. She added a new idea—"eat hot dogs and tacos." Later, she may make further changes.

Planning Your Paragraph Write at least six notes about a special place or event you remember. This could be a fair, an amusement park, a ball park, a circus, or any special event you have attended. Think of things you did or ideas you have about the place or event. Then read your notes. Decide on the main idea. Write it at the bottom. Cross out any notes that do not fit with your main idea, and add any new ideas.

_____

_____

_____

_____

_____

Writing a Draft

Writing a Paragraph
46

Once you have planned your paragraph, you are ready to write a draft. A **draft** is your first try at writing your paragraph. In a draft, you turn your notes into sentences. Follow these steps to write your draft.

1. Read the main idea you wrote below your notes. Write a sentence that clearly tells the main idea. This is your topic sentence.
2. Write at least one full sentence about each of your ideas.
3. If you think of more things to say, add them to your list. Then write sentences about your new ideas.

This is the topic sentence Becky wrote:

You can have a wonderful time at our school carnival.

Then she wrote a sentence about each of her notes. This is what she wrote. She will improve it later.

The PTA runs the carnival. You can play all kinds of games and win prizes. You can try to win a goldfish. At the Treasure Chest you always get something special. If you feel brave, you can go through the haunted house. You can buy hot dogs or tacos to eat.

Writing a Paragraph Look back at the notes and the main idea you wrote about your special place or event. Write a topic sentence below that clearly tells your main idea. Then, on a sheet of paper, copy the topic sentence and write a full sentence about each of your notes. If you think of more ideas, add notes about them to your list. Then write sentences about your new ideas. Save this paragraph for a later exercise.

Topic Sentence: _____

_____

_____

Revising a Paragraph

After you have written your paragraph, you may want to make changes to make the paragraph better. This is called **revising** a paragraph. The following questions will help you revise your paragraph.

> **Guides for Revising**
> 1. Is the paragraph easy to understand?
> 2. Is every group of words a sentence?
> 3. Do all the sentences tell about the main idea? Should any sentences be taken out? Does the paragraph need more sentences to make it clearer? Do any sentences need more words?

Becky thought about ways to improve her paragraph. She took out a sentence that did not fit. She added words to explain her ideas better. She added an ending sentence. Notice the changes she made.

You can have a wonderful time at our school carnival. ~~The PTA runs the carnival.~~ You can play all kinds of games and win prizes. *The prizes are toys or stuffed animals.* You can try to win a goldfish. At the Treasure Chest you always get something special. If you feel brave, you can go through the *scary* haunted house. You can ~~buy~~ *eat delicious* hot dogs or *spicy* tacos ~~to eat~~. *The carnival is so much fun!*

Revising a Paragraph Rewrite the following paragraph correctly on your own paper. If a group of words is not a sentence, add words to make it complete. If a group does not belong in the paragraph, leave it out. **Answers will vary slightly. A suggested answer is given.**

Kangaroos are fascinating animals. They huge feet and long tails. Move around by hopping. I saw some kangaroos on television last week. Mother kangaroos carry their babies in pouches. Live in Australia.

Kangaroos are fascinating animals. They have huge feet and long tails. They move around by hopping. Mother kangaroos carry their babies in pouches. Kangaroos live in Australia.

Revising Your Draft Read carefully the draft of the paragraph you wrote about your special place or event. Ask yourself the questions under the Guides for Revising above. Think of ways to improve your paragraph. Add or cross out words or sentences as necessary.

Proofreading a Paragraph

Writing a Paragraph 48

Proofreading is part of revising. When you proofread, you check for mistakes in grammar, capitalization, punctuation, and spelling. These guides will help you proofread your paragraph.

Guides for Proofreading	
GRAMMAR	When you use pronouns, is it clear whom you are talking about?
CAPITAL LETTERS	Does every sentence and every proper noun begin with a capital letter?
PUNCTUATION	Does every sentence have the correct end mark?
SPELLING	Are all the words spelled correctly?

As you read your paragraph, use these symbols to mark your mistakes.

Symbols for Revising and Proofreading

SYMBOL	EXAMPLE	MEANING	CORRECTION
≡	c	Capitalize a letter.	C
/	D	Change a capital letter to lower case.	d
∧	realy	Add letters or words.	really
—	writeing	Leave something out.	writing
⊙	Dr	Add a period.	Dr.
∽	freind	Trade places.	friend
¶		Begin a new paragraph.	

Proofreading a Paragraph This paragraph has been revised and proofread. Rewrite the paragraph on another sheet of paper, making the corrections. Use the chart above to understand the symbols.

Penguins are remarkable. they look like people wearing Tuxedos. most penguins live in very cold areas near the south pole. They look clumsy when they waddle around land they are gracful when they are swimming in teh water.

Penguins are remarkable. They look like people wearing tuxedos. Most penguins live in very cold areas near the South Pole. They look clumsy when they waddle around on land. They are graceful when they swim in the water.

Proofreading Your Paragraph Read your paragraph carefully, looking for mistakes in grammar, capitalization, punctuation, and spelling. Use the symbols above to mark your corrections. Then copy your paragraph in your neatest handwriting. Plan to share your finished work.

Review: Writing a Paragraph

Understanding Paragraphs Read each paragraph. Underline the topic sentence of each one. Decide what the main idea is.

1. <u>Sweet corn is my favorite vegetable.</u> I like to eat it on the cob with butter. It tastes sweet and juicy, and it is fun to eat. Sometimes I eat across the row, and sometimes I eat around the cob.

   What is the main idea? <u>**why sweet corn is the writer's favorite vegetable**</u>

2. <u>Corey was nervous about his first day at the new school.</u> He did not know any of the other children. The maze of hallways and stairs confused him. He wished he were back at his old school.

   What is the main idea? <u>**Corey's nervousness on the first day of school**</u>

Revising a Paragraph Read the following paragraph. Revise and proofread it, using the symbols you have learned. Then copy the paragraph, making the corrections on the lines below.

   It is important to exercise. exercise keeps your body healthy it makes yuo feel good. Exercising gives you Energy to your Work. also keeps your body fit trim.

   It is important to exercise. Exercise keeps your body healthy.

   It makes you feel good. Exercising gives you energy to do your work.

   It also keeps your body fit and trim.

Verbs That Tell About Present Time

Managing Verb Forms
50

Some verbs tell about things that are happening right now. We say verbs like this are in the **present tense**.

Verbs have two forms to show action in the present. One form, called the **basic form,** is the verb by itself. Examples are *talk* and *read*. The other form, the **-s form,** is the basic form with an *s* added. Examples are *talks* and *reads*.

If the subject of the sentence is singular, use the -s form.

Bernita *grows* vegetables.

If the subject is plural, use the basic form. Also, use the basic form if the subject is *I* or *you*.

Bernita and Alex *grow* vegetables.   I *grow* vegetables.

Add *-es,* instead of *-s,* to verbs that end in *s, x, z, ch,* or *sh*.

push—pushes   munch—munches

If a verb ends in *y* following a consonant, change the *y* to *i,* and add *-es.*

marry—marries   worry—worries

Using Verbs That Tell About the Present Underline the correct verb form in the parentheses.

1. Both seals and otters (<u>swim</u>, swims) well.
2. Some people (<u>carry</u>, carries) their money in a money belt.
3. This sticky strip (catch, <u>catches</u>) flying bugs.
4. The circus horses (<u>prance</u>, prances) to the music.
5. You (<u>write</u>, writes) interesting stories.
6. The bee (buzz, <u>buzzes</u>) around the flowers.
7. I (<u>brush</u>, brushes) my teeth several times a day.
8. Grandfather (teach, <u>teaches</u>) us how to whittle.
9. That crust (taste, <u>tastes</u>) like paper.
10. The loud rumbling (scare, <u>scares</u>) me.
11. Tadpoles (<u>grow</u>, grows) into frogs.
12. A conductor (punch, <u>punches</u>) the tickets.
13. A carpenter (need, <u>needs</u>) a level to check surfaces.
14. Your shirt (match, <u>matches</u>) your jacket.
15. We (<u>hurry</u>, hurries) through our chores on Fridays.

Verbs That Tell About the Past

Managing Verb Forms
51

Some verbs tell about things that have already happened. We say verbs like this are in the **past tense**. To make most verbs show past time, add *-ed* to the basic form.

    jump—jumped   wash—washed

If a verb has a single vowel followed by a single consonant, double the final consonant before adding *-ed.*

    hop—hopped   tap—tapped

If a verb ends in silent *e,* drop the final *e* before adding *-ed.*

    like—liked   skate—skated

If a verb ends in *y* following a consonant, change the *y* to *i* before adding *-ed.*

    marry—married   worry—worried

Forming Verbs with the *-ed* Ending After each verb, write its *-ed* form.

1. pick   **picked**
2. close   **closed**
3. carry   **carried**
4. pave   **paved**
5. wait   **waited**
6. mop   **mopped**

Using Helping Verbs Another way to show past time is to use helping verbs with the *-ed* form of the verb.

    she has jumped   they have washed

When the subject is singular, use the helping verb *has,* as in *she has jumped.* When the subject is plural, use *have,* as in *they have worked.* Also use *have* when the subject is *I* or *you.* Use *had* with either a singular or plural subject.

Using Verbs That Tell About the Past Underline the correct verb.

1. The artist (<u>has painted</u>, have painted) his initials.
2. Six runners (has jogged, <u>have jogged</u>) along the river.
3. The fisherman (<u>has used</u>, have used) a sparkling lure.
4. Most of the apples (has dropped, <u>had dropped</u>) from the trees.
5. I (has polished, <u>have polished</u>) the silver platter.

Irregular Verbs

To make most verbs tell about the past, you add an *-ed* ending. Verbs that form the past tense in this way are called **regular** verbs.

Some verbs do not show past action by adding *-ed* to the basic form. They are called **irregular** verbs. Some of these verbs change their entire form to show past time. For example, *bring* becomes *brought*. Some irregular verbs change their form again to show past time with a helping verb. Notice how *break* changes.

   break   broke   has broken

Here are some irregular verbs:

PRESENT	PAST ALONE	PAST WITH HELPING VERB
bring	brought	(have) brought
come	came	(have) come
do	did	(have) done
eat	ate	(have) eaten
give	gave	(have) given
go	went	(have) gone
run	ran	(have) run
see	saw	(have) seen
take	took	(have) taken
throw	threw	(have) thrown

Using Irregular Verbs Underline the correct verb form.

1. Brad has (ate, <u>eaten</u>) the last peach.
2. The clown (<u>gave</u>, given) balloons to the children.
3. Erica has (went, <u>gone</u>) to Cleveland.
4. Sasha (brung, <u>brought</u>) some shells from the beach.
5. The guests have (came, <u>come</u>) on time.
6. Mom and Dad (<u>did</u>, done) the grocery shopping.
7. The plane has (took, <u>taken</u>) off.
8. The pitcher (<u>threw</u>, throwed) the ball to second base.
9. Our car had (ran, <u>run</u>) out of gas.
10. Emil (<u>saw</u>, seen) a shooting star last night.

Mixed Practice: Managing Verb Forms

Using Verbs That Tell About the Present In the blank, write the present tense form of the verb in the parentheses. Use the correct form to match the subject.

1. A starfish __sees__ (see) the world from eyes on its arms.

2. Lobsters __swim__ (swim) by wiggling their tails.

3. The pelican __flies__ (fly) low to catch fish.

4. Jamie usually __catches__ (catch) the most fish.

5. Anteaters sometimes __eat__ (eat) termites for breakfast.

Using Verbs That Tell About the Past Underline the correct verb from the parentheses.

1. The scared armadillo (<u>had curled</u>, have curled) into a ball.

2. The pandas (<u>ate</u>, eaten) bamboo plants for supper.

3. We have (saw, <u>seen</u>) many ladybugs.

4. Jeff (taped, <u>tapped</u>) his pencil to the drum beats.

5. Several infants (cryed, <u>cried</u>) themselves to sleep.

6. A small snake (<u>has swallowed</u>, have swallowed) the frog.

7. The sun has (<u>come</u>, came) out again after heavy rains.

8. Bees (brung, <u>brought</u>) nectar back to the honeycomb.

9. What have you (did, <u>done</u>)?

10. The audience (claped, <u>clapped</u>) a long time.

11. Someone has (gave, <u>given</u>) a doll to the monkey.

12. Dawn (<u>saw</u>, seen) a sailboat from the shore.

13. Andrew (droped, <u>dropped</u>) the anchor into the water.

14. Elephants (<u>have taken</u>, has taken) leaves from the trees.

15. He has (<u>gone</u>, went) down the waterslide.

Using Verbs in Writing

Managing Verb Forms

Write both past tense forms of each verb below.

	PAST	PAST WITH HELPING VERB
1. cry	cried	cried
2. go	went	gone
3. see	saw	seen
4. trap	trapped	trapped
5. run	ran	run
6. discover	discovered	discovered

Now pretend that you are a jungle explorer. Yesterday you had an exciting day. Write a paragraph that tells what happened in the jungle yesterday. Use the past form of at least three verbs from the list above.

_____
_____
_____
_____
_____
_____
_____
_____
_____
_____

Review: Managing Verb Forms

Using Verbs That Tell About the Present Underline the correct verb form in the parentheses.

1. Turtles (<u>bury</u>, buries, burys) their eggs in the sand.
2. The nurse (check, <u>checks</u>) your blood pressure.
3. Many birds (<u>fly</u>, flies) south for the winter.
4. You (<u>bring</u>, brings) pickle relish to the picnic.
5. Many bugs (<u>live</u>, lives) in dead trees.
6. Courtney (enjoy, <u>enjoys</u>) crossword puzzles.
7. I (<u>hear</u>, hears) the crickets at night.
8. Helicopters (<u>land</u>, lands) on top of that building.
9. Bamboo shoots (<u>grow</u>, grows) very quickly.
10. My father (rise, <u>rises</u>) at dawn.

Using Verbs That Tell About the Past Write the correct form of the verb called for in parentheses.

Answer	Sentence
have *or* had come	1. Two team members (come—past with helping verb) onto the field.
carried	2. The mother opossum (carry—past) her youngsters on her back.
saw	3. We (see—past) the skull of a bison on the plain.
has *or* had done	4. The ballet dancer (do—past with helping verb) her exercises.
has *or* had shouted	5. Someone (shout—past with helping verb) for help.
brought	6. You (bring—past) the wrong jar.
tagged	7. The catcher (tag—past) the runner out.
have *or* had gone	8. Most of the fish (go—past with helping verb) to deeper water.
ate	9. Marjorie (eat—past) lunch at my house.
have *or* had planted	10. Doug and Denny (plant—past with helping verb) the seeds.

Thinking About a Narrative

Writing a Narrative 56

A **narrative** tells a story. The story can be real or make-believe. The narrative can be about yourself or others. Read the following narrative.

> Last night I went to a Halloween birthday party. Everyone at the party was given a list of things we had to find in my friend's back yard. It was dark outside, and the things were hard to find. We all searched and found little skeletons, pumpkins, fake fingers, false teeth, and plastic spiders. Then we each had to find part of a scarecrow's body. My friend and I found the legs, and we brought them to the basement. When everybody found their parts, we put the scarecrow together. It was scary, but so much fun!

Studying a Narrative Reread the paragraph above. Then answer the following questions.

1. Could this story really happen or is it make-believe? __could really happen__

2. The **characters** are the people or animals in the story. Is the writer a character in this narrative?
   __yes__

3. The **setting** is where the narrative takes place. Where did this narrative take place?
   __a friend's back yard__

Now read a different kind of story.

> Val raced into the jungle just ahead of the giant Blob. The Blob had no trouble chasing him through the thick trees. It separated around the trees and then reformed on the other side of them. Val panted as he dodged thick vines and tore through high grasses. He saw the river ahead even as he heard the Blob catching up to him. He dived into the river. The Blob followed, just as Val had hoped. Val was safe at last! The warm river water dissolved the huge Blob into nothing.

Thinking About Stories Reread the paragraph above. Then answer the following questions.

1. Who are the characters in this story? __Val, the Blob__

2. Is this story real or made up? __made up__

3. What is the setting of the story? __a jungle near a river__

4. The **plot** is what happens in the story. What happened in this story?
   __The Blob chased Val through the jungle. Val dived into river. The Blob followed him into the river. The Blob dissolved in the water.__

Prewriting: Planning a Narrative

Writing a Narrative
57

The first step in planning a narrative is to choose an idea for a story and plan the characters and setting. You can write about a real event or make up a story from your imagination. The characters in your narrative can be yourself, other people, or animals. You must think about where and when the narrative happens.

After you decide on your characters and setting, list all the things that happened. If the event really happened, remember the order in which it happened. If you are making up a story, decide what happens. Put those things in the order you choose. Plan a beginning, middle, and end for your narrative.

Making Prewriting Notes Choose one of the following story ideas. Circle it. Make prewriting notes to plan a story. Make notes about the characters, setting, and things that happen in the story. **Notes will vary.**

1. Someone survives a terrible storm
2. Someone finds a long-lost pet
3. Someone discovers an unusual plant

Characters _____

_____

Setting _____

What Happens _____

_____

_____

_____

_____

_____

Prewriting: Planning Your Narrative Choose an idea for your own narrative. You may use the idea you chose from the list above, or you may choose a new idea. Make notes about your characters and setting. Then list the events in the order they happen. Make a prewriting plan. **Plans will vary.**

Skills Practice Book, Aqua Level
Copyright © by McDougal, Littell & Company

Writing a Draft

Writing a Narrative
58

Use your writing plan to write a draft of your story. Your first sentence should catch the reader's interest. It can begin to tell the story. It can also introduce the characters and setting. The rest of your sentences should tell the story in the order that it happened.

You might need more than one paragraph to tell the story. Indent and start a new paragraph if you have a natural break in the action. You might want to separate the beginning, middle, and end of the story.

Use time words to help your reader understand when things happen. These are words and phrases like *first, then, next, a few hours later, the next day, finally, in the morning,* and *that night.*

Using Time Words Fill in the following paragraph with time words to help the reader follow the order of the story. Here are some time words you can choose from. **Answers will vary. Suggested answers are given.**

then	one day	suddenly
next	the next day	all at once
finally	Tuesday	a little later

Last week, Tony and I spent several days examining plants and animals in the woods. **One day**, it rained. **The next day**, we saw what looked like a clump of moving jelly crawling slowly over the logs and leaves. **Suddenly**, it stopped moving and began to dry up. By this time the sun was up and the day had turned hot. **Then**, the jelly stuff changed into little balls. **Finally**, the balls burst open and seedlike things flew out. Mom told me that what we saw was a slime mold, which is really a crowd of tiny, living creatures all stuck together. All I know is that I wouldn't want to see that stuff in my lunchbox.

Writing Your Draft Write a good beginning sentence for your own narrative. Then follow your writing plan to write the rest of the story. Add time words where they are needed.

Revising and Proofreading a Narrative

Writing a Narrative 59

After you have written your narrative, look for ways to revise and improve it. Make sure you have told the whole story. Perhaps you can make the story more exciting. Ask yourself these questions.

Guides for Revising
1. Did I describe the setting and characters clearly?
2. Does my story have a beginning, middle, and end?
3. Have I told all the events in the order they happened?
4. Have I added time words to make the time of action clear?

After revising your paragraph for ideas, proofread it for mistakes. Ask yourself these questions.

Guides for Proofreading
1. Did I add commas after time words when they came first in the sentence?
2. Are the verbs in the past tense formed correctly?
3. Are my sentences correctly capitalized and punctuated?
4. Are all words spelled correctly?

Revising Rewrite this paragraph correctly on your own paper. The changes have been marked for you with proofreading marks. **See answer below.**

¶ By accident, I ~~accidentally~~ knocked over Mom's best ˄crystal vase when no one was home. I got out the quick gl~~u~~ed to fix it. ~~B~~before anyone found out. As I dabbed ~~G~~glue on the vase, I spilled some on my ~~F~~fingers. ⎡Just then Mom returned.⎤ Suddenly two fingers stuck together. She was able to unglue me ~~and~~, glue her vase, *and still keep smiling*.

Revising and Proofreading Your Narrative Read your narrative carefully. Look for ways to improve it. Use the two sets of guides above to help. Mark the changes to be made. Then copy your corrected narrative neatly.

By accident, I knocked over Mom's best crystal vase when no one was home. I got out the quick glue to fix it before anyone found out. As I dabbed glue on the vase, I spilled some on my fingers. Suddenly, two fingers stuck together. Just then Mom returned. She was able to unglue me, glue her vase, and still keep smiling.

Review: Writing a Narrative

Writing a Narrative 60

Thinking About a Narrative Read the following narrative. Then answer the questions below.

> On Saturday, I ran in a relay race on the high school track. Three other runners were on my team. We had practiced very hard. My family was there to cheer, and I was nervous. The first runner ran well and handed me the baton. I started out really fast. Just as I passed another runner, I tripped and fell. Everybody passed me while I got up and hobbled to my teammate. I felt so sorry. My teammates caught up to win second place. We would have won first place if I had not fallen.

1. Could this story really happen or is it make-believe? **could really happen**

2. Is the writer a character in this story? **yes**

3. What is the setting of the story? **high school track**

4. Tell what happened in the order it happened.
   First runner handed the writer the baton; writer started to pass another racer and fell; other racers passed writer; writer hobbled to teammate; team came in second.

Revising and Proofreading Rewrite each sentence below correctly. Correct mistakes in grammar, capitalization, punctuation, and spelling. Then circle any time words in the corrected sentences. **Answers may vary slightly.**

1. Sudenly the brite lights started flashing.

   (**Suddenly,**) the bright lights started flashing.

2. The next day our parrents in an old beat-up van.

   (**The next day,**) our parents came in an old beat-up van.

3. Then Jill forced the animal back in the box she shut the lid.

   (**Then,**) Jill forced the animal back in the box. She shut the lid.

4. Finaly the last Racer crosed the finish Line.

   (**Finally,**) the last racer crossed the finish line.

5. that night the witch sung the twins to sleep

   (**That night,**) the witch sang the twins to sleep.

What Are Adjectives?

Understanding Adjectives

An adjective is a word that describes a noun or a pronoun. Because adjectives change, or **modify**, the meaning of a noun, they are also called modifiers. Here is an example.

> I wore boots.
> I wore **new** boots.

The adjective *new* changes the way you see the noun *boots*.

An adjective may come before or after the word it describes. In the following sentences, the adjective *hard* modifies the noun *shell*.

> My turtle has a hard shell.   My turtle's shell is hard.

Usually, when we use two or more adjectives together, we separate them with commas. Adjectives telling *how many* do not follow this rule.

> Four hot, tired runners sat in the shade.

Finding Adjectives In each pair of sentences below, only the adjectives change. Circle the noun that is modified. Then underline all the adjectives in each sentence.

1. <u>Happy</u>, <u>noisy</u> (fans) cheered.
   <u>Sixteen</u> <u>cold</u> (fans) cheered.

2. Jon found <u>smooth</u>, <u>black</u> (fossils.)
   Jon found <u>several</u> <u>interesting</u> (fossils.)

3. Dad collects <u>big</u>, <u>comfortable</u> (chairs.)
   Dad collects <u>antique</u>, <u>wooden</u> (chairs.)

4. <u>Two</u> <u>thirsty</u> (boys) drank lemonade.
   <u>Hot</u>, <u>tired</u> (boys) drank lemonade.

5. Emily has <u>two</u> <u>furry</u> (dogs.)
   Emily has <u>some</u> <u>huge</u> (dogs.)

Using Adjectives Fill in each blank with one or more adjectives. **Adjectives will vary.**

1. Connie has _____ hair.

2. Eric paints _____ pictures.

3. I saw _____ birds.

4. Popcorn tastes _____.

5. _____ monsters scare me.

Three Kinds of Adjectives

Understanding Adjectives

62

Almost every adjective can be placed in one of three groups.

What Kind Some adjectives tell *what kind.* Here are some adjectives in this group:

    juicy   hard   hot   brown   empty

How Many Some adjectives tell *how many.* Some of these tell exactly how many, such as *three* or *seven.* Other adjectives do not tell exact numbers. Examples are *many* and *some.*

Which Ones Some adjectives tell *which ones.* Here are four adjectives of this group that we use often:

    this   that   these   those

These four adjectives always come before the words they modify.

Recognizing Adjectives Find the adjectives in each sentence. Draw one line under adjectives that tell *what kind.* Draw two lines under adjectives that tell *how many.* Circle adjectives that tell *which ones.*

1. <u><u>Some</u></u> clowns have <u>funny</u> faces.
2. <u><u>Three</u></u> <u>huge</u> whales were stranded in <u>shallow</u> water.
3. <u><u>Some</u></u> magicians perform <u>amazing</u> tricks.
4. (That) <u>tall</u> waitress carried <u><u>four</u></u> glasses.
5. <u><u>One</u></u> <u>small</u> boy picked (this) flower.
6. <u><u>Several</u></u> birds flew toward the <u>ripe</u> berries.
7. (These) caterpillars will become <u>beautiful</u> butterflies.
8. <u><u>Six</u></u> artists painted (this) mural.
9. Janet has <u><u>two</u></u> <u>older</u> sisters.
10. <u>Yellow</u> ribbons were tied around (those) trees.

Using Adjectives Add at least three adjectives to the following sentence. Use all three kinds of adjectives. **Adjectives will vary.**

    Dogs bark at squirrels.

Using *A*, *An*, and *The*

Understanding Adjectives
63

The words *a*, *an*, and *the* make a special group of adjectives. They are called **articles**. Follow these rules when you use them.

1. *The* may be used before singular or plural nouns that begin with any letter.

   the artist   *the* robots

2. *A* and *an* are used only before singular nouns.
Use *a* before words beginning with consonant sounds.

   a car   *a* red apple

Use *an* before words beginning with vowel sounds.

   an apple   *an* old car

Some words begin with a silent *h*. The first sound in those words is the vowel sound after the *h*. Therefore, use *an* with silent *h* words.

   an honor   *an* honest opinion

Using *A* and *An* Fill in each blank with **a** or **an**.

1. The hen laid ____**an**____ enormous egg.

2. We elected ____**an**____ honest mayor.

3. One chimpanzee peeled ____**a**____ banana.

4. Annette fed ____**an**____ elephant at the zoo.

5. Jack mailed ____**a**____ postcard to his friend.

6. Two koalas hid in ____**a**____ tree.

7. I heard ____**an**____ owl hoot.

8. David wanted ____**an**____ ice cube for his drink.

9. Abby listened to ____**a**____ new record.

10. Earth travels in ____**an**____ orbit around the sun.

Understanding Adjectives

Using Adjectives To Compare

64

When we compare nouns, we see how they are alike and how they are different. We can use adjectives to compare.

When you compare two people, places, or things, you usually add *-er* to the adjective. When you compare three or more, you usually add *-est*.

A bird is *small*.   A butterfly is *smaller* than a bird.
An ant is the *smallest* of the three animals.

Follow these spelling rules before adding *-er* or *-est*.

1. If a word ends in a single consonant following a single vowel, double the final consonant before adding the ending. Example: *hot, hotter, hottest*

2. If a word ends in silent *e*, drop the final *e* before adding the ending. Example: *nice, nicer, nicest*

3. If a word ends in *y* following a consonant, change the *y* to *i* before adding the ending. Example: *happy, happier, happiest*

When you make comparisons with longer adjectives, use *more* and *most*. Use *more* when you compare two things. Use *most* when you compare three or more things. Do not use *-er* or *-est* and *more* or *most* at the same time.

Good **and *bad* change to completely new words when they are used to compare things.**

good   better   best   bad   worse   worst

Using Adjectives To Compare Write the two forms each adjective uses in making comparisons.

1. kind — kinder — kindest
2. sad — sadder — saddest
3. scary — scarier — scariest
4. beautiful — more beautiful — most beautiful
5. good — better — best
6. silly — sillier — silliest
7. big — bigger — biggest
8. grateful — more grateful — most grateful
9. happy — happier — happiest
10. thin — thinner — thinnest

Mixed Practice: Understanding Adjectives

Understanding Adjectives **65**

Finding Adjectives and the Nouns They Modify Use another sheet of paper for the answers to this exercise. Make four columns with these headings: *What Kind, How Many, Which Ones,* and *Noun Modified.* Find the adjectives in each sentence and write them in the correct columns. Put only one adjective on each line. You may have more than one adjective for each sentence. In the fourth column, write the noun modified by that adjective.

WK = What Kind; HM = How Many; WO = Which Ones; Underscore = Noun Modified.

1. (HM) Three fish swim in that (WO) tank.
2. (WK) Do black cats bring bad luck. (WK)
3. (HM) Many students wrote scary (WK) stories.
4. (WO) That music is loud.
5. (WO) Those teachers planned this (WO) special (WK) trip.
6. (HM) Six close friends formed a secret (WK) club.
7. (WO) Wear these red (WK) boots on rainy (WK) days.
8. (WO) Those tiny (WK) kittens are hungry.
9. (WO) This bookbag is full.
10. (WO) That family owns three (HM) noisy (WK) dogs.

Using Adjectives Correctly Read each sentence. Underline the correct form in the parentheses.

1. Camille ate (a, **an**) apricot.

2. That is the (**tallest**, most tallest) building in the city.

3. The peach is (ripest, **riper**) than the nectarine.

4. (A, **An**) octopus has eight legs.

5. Your handwriting is (**better**, more good) than mine.

6. Smokey is the (**fastest**, faster) of the five colts.

7. We will exercise (a, **the**) horses today.

8. Emily delivered (an, **a**) dozen newspapers.

9. Of the two beds, this one is (**more comfortable**, comfortabler).

10. Who is the (most best, **best**) tennis player in the world?

11. Mr. Taylor planted (a, **an**) evergreen tree.

12. The zookeeper cleaned (a, **the**) cages.

13. This is the (**most colorful**, more colorful) painting in the museum.

14. The ghost wrote with (a, **an**) invisible pen.

15. My toothache is (worst, **worse**) today than it was yesterday.

Using Adjectives in Writing

Understanding Adjectives

66

Read this paragraph.

    I have a <u>nice</u> friend. We always play <u>good</u> games. We like to ride our <u>new</u> bikes. We take our <u>little</u> dogs out for walks. On Saturdays, we go to the store and buy <u>big</u> sundaes. My friends and I have <u>good</u> times together.

Underline every adjective in the paragraph except *a, an,* and *the.* Do these adjectives make the paragraph interesting to read? Are there other adjectives that can tell more about the nouns in the paragraph?

On the lines below, write the paragraph again. Use new adjectives to tell more about the nouns. Make the paragraph more interesting to read. **Paragraphs will vary.**

Review: Understanding Adjectives

Recognizing Three Kinds of Adjectives Underline each adjective. Decide which kind it is, and put a check under the correct heading.

	WHAT KIND	HOW MANY	WHICH ONES	
1.			✔	Marcus watches <u>this</u> program.
2.		✔		Rita has collected <u>many</u> stamps.
3.	✔			Peanuts are <u>salty</u>.
4.			✔	Timmy sorted <u>these</u> papers.
5.		✔		<u>Few</u> children dislike cartoons.

Using A and An Fill in each blank with *a* or *an*.

1. I wish I had **an** umbrella.
2. This is **an** easy problem.
3. Elena hit **a** home run.
4. Shannon wore **a** new hat.
5. There is **an** icicle hanging from our roof.

Comparing People or Things Underline the correct form in the parentheses.

1. That was the (beautifulest, <u>most beautiful</u>) sunset we have ever seen.
2. The sun seems (<u>brighter</u>, brightest) in summer than in winter.
3. Our grandfather clock is (<u>taller</u>, more taller) than my father.
4. This show is (gooder, <u>better</u>) than that one.
5. Of all the flavors, chocolate is the (more delicious, <u>most delicious</u>).
6. Your box is (<u>heavier</u>, more heavier) than mine.
7. Swimming is the (better, <u>best</u>) sport of all.
8. Charles's report is the (<u>neatest</u>, neater) in the class.
9. This corner is (dangerouser, <u>more dangerous</u>) than that one.
10. Today I made the (worse, <u>worst</u>) mistake I have ever made.

What Are Adverbs?

Understanding Adverbs
68

An adverb is a word that modifies, or adds meaning to, a verb or an adjective. Adverbs tell *how*, *where*, or *when*.

HOW	Jenny ran *quickly*.
WHERE	Jenny ran *outside*.
WHEN	Jenny ran *yesterday*.

Many adverbs are formed by adding *-ly* to adjectives.

ADJECTIVE	+	**ly**	=	ADVERB
slow	+	ly	=	slowly
loud	+	ly	=	loudly

Finding Adverbs Underline the adverb in each sentence.

1. Kurt sings <u>well</u>.
2. The rain made us stay <u>inside</u>.
3. I <u>often</u> help Grandmother at her store.
4. The dancer moved <u>gracefully</u>.
5. The wind is howling <u>outside</u>.
6. <u>Tonight</u> we invited a special guest to dinner.
7. Gordon answered the phone <u>sleepily</u>.
8. Don left his library books <u>here</u>.
9. Maureen and Debby <u>never</u> argue.
10. Chris <u>angrily</u> slammed the screen door.

Using Adverbs Add an adverb of any kind to each sentence below.
  Adverbs will vary.

1. Eileen ate her popcorn _____.
2. One horse ran _____.
3. The professor talked _____.
4. Carl climbed the hill _____.
5. The mother lion crept _____.

Recognizing Adverbs

Understanding Adverbs
69

Many adverbs end in *ly*. They are usually made by taking an adjective and adding *-ly* to it. This kind of adverb usually tells *how*.

  quiet + ly = quietly

When the adjective used to form the adverb ends in *y*, we must change the *y* to *i* before adding *-ly*.

  noisy + ly = noisily

Many adverbs do not end in *ly*. They usually tell *where* or *when*.

  here, there, near, outside   now, soon, yesterday, often
  (adverbs that tell *where*)   (adverbs that tell *when*)

Finding Adverbs That Tell *How* Complete each sentence with the adverb that tells *how*.

1. Margaret washed the clothes _____**carefully**_____. (downstairs, yesterday, carefully)

2. They _____**carelessly**_____ left their shoes behind. (carelessly, outside, often)

3. _____**Quickly**_____, Aaron drew a large star. (Upstairs, Quickly, Today)

4. The children ran _____**rudely**_____ through the house. (frequently, everywhere, rudely)

5. This boat was built _____**well**_____. (here, well, Friday)

Using Adverbs That Tell *Where* and *When* In the following sentences, draw one line under the adverbs that tell *where*. Draw two lines under the adverbs that tell *when*.

1. Kent will bake cookies <u>here</u> <u><u>tomorrow</u></u>.

2. Our laundry room is <u>downstairs</u> <u><u>now</u></u>.

3. <u><u>First</u></u>, we must paint each piece <u>outside</u>.

4. <u><u>Later</u></u> we will take the flag <u>down</u>.

5. Grandpa will be leaving <u>here</u> <u><u>soon</u></u>.

6. <u><u>Frequently</u></u> Ernest preferred to stay <u>indoors</u>.

7. The birds <u><u>never</u></u> come to eat <u>here</u>.

8. The neighbors <u><u>sometimes</u></u> picnic <u>there</u>.

Using Adverbs To Compare

Understanding Adverbs
70

Adverbs, like adjectives, can be used to show **comparisons.** There are three ways adverbs are changed to show comparisons.

1. Some short adverbs add *-er* to compare the actions of two people or things. They add *-est* to compare three or more.

    fast   faster   fastest

2. Most adverbs that end in *ly* use the word *more* to compare the actions of two people or things. They use *most* in comparing three or more.

    quietly   more quietly   most quietly

3. Some adverbs change their forms completely in comparisons.

    well better best   badly worse worst

Making the Forms of Adverbs
Write the two forms each adverb uses in making comparisons.

1. soon   **sooner**   **soonest**
2. happily   **more happily**   **most happily**
3. badly   **worse**   **worst**
4. unevenly   **more unevenly**   **most unevenly**
5. often   **more often**   **most often**

Using Adverbs To Make Comparisons
Underline the correct adverb form.

1. Derek patted the dog (<u>more gently</u>, gentlier) than Betsy.
2. Kevin acts (<u>more confidently</u>, most confidently) than I do.
3. The lion growled (more fiercely, <u>most fiercely</u>) of all the cats.
4. My ankle hurts (<u>worse</u>, worser) than my knee.
5. Gina skates (<u>better</u>, best) than Paula.
6. Can a fish swim (<u>faster</u>, more fast) than a turtle?
7. The bulbs were buried (<u>deeper</u>, more deeper) than we thought.
8. Mr. Fong answered (more quickly, <u>most quickly</u>) of the whole group.
9. My brother walks (<u>more quietly</u>, quietlier) than my sister.
10. Play this section (slowlier, <u>more slowly</u>) than that section.

Mixed Practice: Understanding Adverbs

Recognizing Adverbs Underline the adverb in each sentence. In the blank, write whether the adverb tells *how, where,* or *when*.

1. The boys <u>fearfully</u> climbed the creaking stairs. __how__
2. <u>Then</u> Gayle ran to her bike. __when__
3. The otters swam <u>smoothly</u> through the water. __how__
4. We <u>almost</u> missed the bus. __how__
5. Several white moths flew <u>inside</u>. __where__
6. I have <u>never</u> driven a car. __when__
7. Ron came <u>here</u> for dinner. __where__
8. Wash the windows <u>more carefully</u>. __how__
9. <u>Yesterday</u> Jess missed her viola lesson. __when__
10. Chicken feathers were flying <u>everywhere</u>. __where__

Using Adverbs To Compare Use the correct form of the adverb in parentheses to complete these sentences.

1. Leslie performed __better__ (well) than I did.
2. The lion kitten plays __most roughly__ (roughly) of all these young animals.
3. It snowed __more often__ (often) in April than in February.
4. Without oil, the door will squeak __worse__ (badly) than it does now.
5. Of all the members in the band, the drummers played __most loudly__ (loudly).

Understanding Adverbs

Using Adverbs in Writing

72

Read the list of verbs below. For each verb, write three adverbs that will modify the verb. Remember, adverbs tell *how, when,* and *where.* Try to use all three kinds of adverbs. **Adverbs will vary.**

climbed _____   shouted _____

climbed _____   shouted _____

climbed _____   shouted _____

walked _____   returned _____

walked _____   returned _____

walked _____   returned _____

Now, imagine that you have been climbing a mountain. Write a paragraph that tells about your trip. Try to use an adverb in every sentence you write. You might use some of the verbs and adverbs from the list above. **Paragraphs will vary.**

_____
_____
_____
_____
_____
_____
_____
_____
_____
_____

Review: Understanding Adverbs

Finding Adverbs Underline the adverb in each sentence.

1. Kelly arrived <u>late</u>.
2. Lou carried the tray <u>upstairs</u>.
3. The plane will land <u>soon</u>.
4. <u>Today</u> I am ready.
5. The astronaut walked <u>awkwardly</u> on the moon.
6. Ms. Stokes planted a maple tree <u>here</u>.
7. The dry leaves scattered <u>everywhere</u>.
8. Domingo wrote his science report <u>neatly</u>.
9. My Cub Scout project is <u>almost</u> finished.
10. The red fox hid <u>silently</u> in the bushes.

Using Adverbs Add an adverb of any kind to each sentence below.
   Adverbs will vary.

1. One referee blew her whistle _____.
2. Lightning struck _____.
3. The choir sang _____.
4. Katie answered _____.
5. The sun slipped _____ behind clouds.

Using Adverbs To Make Comparisons Write the two forms each adverb uses to make comparisons.

1. well — better — best
2. early — earlier — earliest
3. cheerfully — more cheerfully — most cheerfully
4. fast — faster — fastest
5. eagerly — more eagerly — most eagerly

Entry Words

Using the Dictionary and Thesaurus

A dictionary gives the meanings and pronunciations of words. Each word listed in the dictionary is called an **entry word.** The entry words in a dictionary are in alphabetical order from *A* to *Z.* If two words begin with the same letter, they are listed in alphabetical order by the second letter. If the second letters are also the same, they are listed alphabetically by their third letter, and so on.

BY FIRST LETTER	BY SECOND LETTER	BY THIRD LETTER
bite	lake	pear
chew	leaf	peck
drink	limb	pencil
eat	lodge	pest

Words that begin with a letter from *A* to *L* are in the first half of the dictionary. Words that begin with a letter from *M* to *Z* are in the second half. Opening your dictionary to the correct half saves you time in looking up a word.

Finding Entry Words Write the words in each group in alphabetical order. Then decide in which half of the dictionary you would find each word in lists 1 and 2. Write **A–L** or **M–Z** beside each word.

1
glass	corner	A–L
mask	glass	A–L
tailor	mask	M–Z
piano	piano	M–Z
corner	tailor	M–Z

3
dive	dance
dog	dive
dust	dog
drop	drop
dance	dust

2
magazine	bank	A–L
bank	borrow	A–L
library	lend	A–L
borrow	library	A–L
lend	magazine	M–Z

4
rise	rich
riddle	riddle
robe	rise
rocker	robe
rich	rocker

Using Guide Words

At the top of every dictionary page are two guide words in heavy, black type. They guide you to the word you want. The guide word at the left is the first entry word on the page. The guide word on the right is the last entry word on that page. All the entry words are in alphabetical order between the two guide words.

Using Guide Words On the left are ten sets of guide words. On the right is a list of entry words. Find an entry word that would come on the same page as each set of guide words. Write that entry word next to the guide words.

1. microphone—mighty __midnight__ fashion
2. bacon—bait __badge__ badge
3. family—farce __fan__ major
4. bluebell—boast __blush__ went
5. mailman—make __major__ twelve
6. turtle—twine __twelve__ midnight
7. well—western __went__ fan
8. gift—give __giraffe__ tuition
9. farthest—fate __fashion__ giraffe
10. tubule—tumor __tuition__ blush

Using the Dictionary Look up each of the following words in a classroom dictionary. Next to each word, copy the guide words that are on the page where you found the word. **Answers depend on dictionary used.**

1. imperial _____
2. rapid _____
3. denote _____
4. oust _____
5. secure _____

Respelling and Pronunciation

The first thing a dictionary tells about an entry word is its pronunciation. The **pronunciation** is the right way to say the word.

In most dictionaries, the entry word is printed in dark, black letters. After the entry word come special letters and marks in parentheses. This is called the **respelling.** The respelling shows the pronunciation of the word. Here is an example.

sys • tem   (sis′ təm)

Every dictionary has a **pronunciation key.** The pronunciation key explains what sounds the letters and marks in the respelling stand for. Here is part of a pronunciation key.

fat,   āpe   cär,   ten,   ēven,   hit,   bīte,   gō

ə = *a* in ago, *e* in agent, *i* in sanity, *o* in confess, *u* in focus

The symbol ə, called *schwa,* is in the respelling of *system.* The pronunciation key tells you that the ə sound is like the *e* in *agent.*

In the respelling, the word is broken into parts. Each part is called a **syllable.** The letters in a syllable are spoken as a group together. The slanted line following a syllable is called an **accent mark.** The accent mark tells you which syllable to say more strongly. In the word *system,* you say the first syllable more strongly.

Finding the Pronunciation Here are five sets of words with their respellings. In each set, two of the three words rhyme with each other because they have the same vowel sound. Underline those two words.

1. <u>drone (drōn)</u>   gone (gôn)   <u>phone (fōn)</u>
2. suave (swäv)   <u>heave (hēv)</u>   <u>relieve (ri lēv′)</u>
3. <u>tour (toor)</u>   <u>pure (pyoor)</u>   scour (skour)
4. <u>plight (plīt)</u>   grit (grit)   <u>byte (bīt)</u>
5. plaid (plad)   <u>staid (stād)</u>   <u>glade (glād)</u>

Finding the Accent Here are some words and their respellings. Find the accent mark. Write which syllable has the accent—**1, 2,** or **3.**

1. enterprise (en′ tər prīz)   __1__
2. harmonica (här män′ i kə)   __2__
3. factory (fak′ tə rē)   __1__
4. safari (sə fä′ rē)   __2__
5. incorrect (in kə rekt′)   __3__

Understanding the Definition

Definitions are the largest part of each dictionary entry. The definition tells what the entry word means.

Some definitions are followed by a sample sentence. The sentence shows one meaning of the word.

Many words have more than one meaning. A dictionary gives all the meanings of each entry word. You may have to choose from more than one meaning to find the one that fits best.

> **stock** (stäk), **n.** **1.** a supply on hand for use or for sale [Our *stock* of food is low.] **2.** livestock; cattle, horses, sheep, pigs, etc. **3.** shares in a business [He bought *stock* in several companies.] **4.** ancestry or family [He is of French *stock*.] **5.** a particular breed of an animal or plant. **6.** water in which meat or fish has been boiled, used to make soup, gravy, etc. **7.** the part that serves as a handle or body for the working parts [The *stock* of a rifle holds the barrel in place.] **8.** a tree trunk or stump.

Finding the Meaning Use the above dictionary entry for *stock*. Write the definition that fits each of the following sentences.

1. Ms. Braden bought stock in a computer company.

   3. shares in a business

2. Add vegetables to the beef stock to make a good soup.

   6. water in which meat or fish has been boiled, used to make soup, gravy, etc.

3. The store has a large stock of school materials.

   1. supply on hand for use or for sale

4. Our new neighbor is of Canadian stock.

   4. ancestry or family

5. A farmer must feed his stock every day.

   2. livestock; cattle, horses, sheep, pigs, etc.

6. The woodcutter chopped the tree down to its stock.

   8. a tree trunk or stump

7. This stock of tulips yields yellow flowers.

   5. a particular breed of an animal or plant

8. The pioneer fitted a new stock on his old shotgun.

   7. the part that serves as a handle or body for the working parts

Synonyms and Antonyms

Using the Dictionary and Thesaurus
78

A dictionary sometimes gives synonyms and antonyms for entry words. **Synonyms** are words that mean almost the same thing. **Antonyms** are words that mean the opposite.

These sets of words are synonyms.

    talk—speak   rich—wealthy   strange—odd

These sets of words are antonyms.

    simple—difficult   weak—powerful   hard—soft

Usually one particular word must exactly fit the meaning you have in mind. Suppose you are describing a strong wind. The wind is so strong it can blow down trees. *Great, powerful, healthy,* and *tough* are all synonyms for *strong.* The synonym that best describes the wind is *powerful.*

Using Synonyms and Antonyms For each numbered entry word, find and write one synonym and one antonym from the words in the box below. Write the words next to the entry words. Use your dictionary if you need help.

Entry Word	Synonym	Antonym
1. fast	swift	slow
2. friend	pal	enemy
3. shiny	bright	dull
4. young	youthful	aged
5. narrow	thin	broad

slow	bright	aged	enemy	pal
swift	thin	broad	dull	youthful

Choosing the Best Synonym In each sentence below, the underlined word can be replaced by one of the synonyms in parentheses. Read the explanation following each sentence. Underline the synonym that best expresses the meaning.

1. This test is hard.   (<u>difficult</u>, harsh)   [It is not easy.]

2. Your cake is good.   (<u>delicious</u>, well-made)   [It is tasty.]

3. A diamond is a precious stone.   (cherished, <u>valuable</u>)   [It is worth much money.]

4. Aaron lost a quarter.   (<u>mislaid</u>, failed)   [He could not find it.]

5. Sarah is always sweet.   (sugary, <u>friendly</u>)   [She is nice to others.]

Using a Thesaurus

Using the Dictionary and Thesaurus

A **thesaurus** is a book or part of a book which lists synonyms and antonyms for many words. The entry words in a thesaurus are sometimes listed in alphabetical order. Sometimes, words might be grouped by category. Usually you can consult the index of the thesaurus to locate the word you want.

The thesaurus is a helpful tool for writing. You can use it to replace a word you have used too often. You can use it to replace a word with one that has a more precise meaning.

Compare these two paragraphs. Notice how changing over-used words improves the paragraph.

> Architects *like* working with shapes and measurements. They also *like* the task of dreaming up new designs and plans for buildings. They especially *like* watching their ideas become reality with the help of a construction crew.

> Architects *like* working with shapes and measurements. They also *enjoy* the task of dreaming up new designs and plans for buildings. They *take* special *pleasure* in watching their ideas become reality with the help of a construction crew.

Using a Thesaurus Use the thesaurus in the **Power Handbook** to find a synonym for each underlined word in these sentences. Write the synonyms.

1. Molly heard strange noises coming from the attic. __mysterious, odd, unusual, peculiar, unfamiliar, wierd__

2. I think you may be wrong about the costume colors. __incorrect, mistaken__

3. Our class is making a model of the Capitol. __building, constructing__

4. We'll need to get some new curtains for this room. __buy, purchase__

5. Eddie saw the missing keys on the floor. __sighted, spotted__

Finding Antonyms Use your thesaurus to replace the underlined words with words that have the opposite meaning. Write the antonyms on the blanks.

1. The bright light made the long hall more scary. __dim__

2. The witch turned out to be a gorgeous creature. __homely, hideous, ugly__

3. Juan was surprised that the reward was so small. __big, enormous, great__

4. Dad was angry with the crowd that had gathered. __happy, pleased__

5. The delivery man was acting in a strange manner. __ordinary__

Mixed Practice: Using the Dictionary and Thesaurus

Using the Dictionary Look up the underlined word from each sentence below **Answers will vary** in your dictionary. Then add this information on the lines. **depending on dictionary used. These answers are taken from *Webster's New World Dictionary*, Student Edition, Simon & Schuster, 1981.**

1. the respelling, showing syllables and the accent mark
2. the meaning that best fits the sentence
3. the guide words on the page where you found the word

1. Our waiter spoke with a French <u>accent</u>.

   (ak′ sent); a distinguishing regional or national way of pronouncing;

   absurd—acceptance

2. We paddled down the south <u>branch</u> of Eagle River.

   (branch); any of the streams into which a river may divide or which flow into it;

   brainstorming—brave

3. Mark <u>dashed</u> across the street to catch the bus.

   (dash); to move swiftly; rush; Daphne—dashboard

4. The ship's <u>company</u> repaired the sails after the storm.

   (kum′ pə nē); the whole crew of a ship, including officers; commune—comparable

5. Janine made a <u>motion</u> that the meeting be adjourned.

   (mō′ shən); a suggestion; esp., a proposal formally made in an assembly or meeting;

   mother—mound

Using the Thesaurus Look up each word below in the thesaurus in the **Power Handbook.** Write two synonyms next to the word.

1. say — cry, explain, grumble, shout, whisper, announce, assert, blurt, boast, comment, declare, growl, remark, roar, state

2. many — countless, several

3. help — aid, assist, rescue

4. big — enormous, gigantic, huge, immense, colossal, great, mammoth, monumental

5. bad — careless, evil, poor, vicious, unsatisfactory

Using the Dictionary in Writing

Look up each word below in a dictionary. Write the meaning of the word next to it.
Answers will vary slightly depending on dictionary used.

1. larva **early, free-living, immature form of an insect or animal that changes in structure when it becomes an adult**

2. pupa **insect in stage between larva and adult forms**

3. caterpillar **wormlike larva of insects**

4. cocoon **silky case which larvae of certain insects spin about themselves for shelter during pupa stage**

Now use the words and information above to write a short paragraph about butterflies. You may use several words in one sentence. **Paragraphs will vary.**

Review: Using the Dictionary and Thesaurus

Using Guide Words On the left are sets of guide words. On the right is a list of entry words. Find an entry word that would come on the same page as each set of guide words. Write that entry word next to the guide words.

1. stole—store   _____stool_____   warp
2. warning—washout   _____warp_____   lime
3. mill—mind   _____mimic_____   sweater
4. limb—line   _____lime_____   mimic
5. swap—sweeping   _____sweater_____   stool

Understanding a Dictionary Entry Read the following section of a dictionary entry. Then answer the questions below about the entry.

> **o·rig·i·nal** (ə rij′ə n′l) *adj.* **1.** having to do with an origin; first; earliest [the *original* inhabitants of an area] **2.** never having been before; new; novel [an *original* idea] **3.** capable of creating something new, or thinking or acting in an independent, fresh way; inventive [an *original* composer] **4.** coming from someone as the originator, maker, author, etc. [an *original* Picasso painting] **5.** being that from which copies, translations, etc. have been made [the *original* letter and two carbons]

1. What is the entry word? _____original_____

2. Under which set of guide words would you find *original*? Underline the correct set.

   ordinal—orient   <u>oriental—orthodontics</u>   orthodox—osmosis

3. How many syllables does the entry word contain? ___4___

4. Which syllable is accented? _____second syllable_____

5. What sample phrase is shown for the first meaning of *original*?

   _____the *original* inhabitants of an area_____

6. Write the number of the meaning that fits each sentence below.

   __5__ a. Put the *original* page face down on the copy machine.
   __1__ b. The *original* settlers built this fort.
   __2__ c. Joe thought of an *original* way to advertise the product.
   __4__ d. This masterpiece is the *original* painting.
   __3__ e. That *original* designer keeps thinking of new styles.

Thinking About Descriptions

Writing a Description
83

A **description** paints a picture with words. As you read, you can "see" what is being described in your mind.

Here is a description. Try to "see" Krista's world in your mind.

> Overnight, Krista's yard turned into a wonderland of snow. She looked out the window at a white lawn sparkling in the sunlight. Thin ribbons of snow decorated the branches of the trees. Little mounds of snow were taking rides on her swings. A huge hat of snow sat on the roof of the car. Everywhere Krista looked, she saw dazzling whiteness.

The description begins with a topic sentence. The rest of the sentences **describe** Krista's yard. They tell what it looked like.

Forming a Picture in Your Mind Read this description carefully. Then, in the space below, draw and color a picture of a gnome. Follow the description.

> The gnome stood stubbornly in the way. He was short and somewhat stout. He had long, gray hair and a long, gray beard. His nose and cheeks were red. On his head sat a bright green hat with a long tassel. The gnome's tight-fitting jacket was a bright green. He wore short, black pants and high, black boots. He stood with one hand on his hip. In the other hand, he held a long staff. He looked at me angrily from under his bushy eyebrows.

Skills Practice Book, Aqua Level
Copyright © by McDougal, Littell & Company

Prewriting: Selecting Details

Writing a Description
84

Often a description is part of a longer piece you are writing, such as a story or a report. You use description to help the reader see a character, place, or an object you have in mind.

At other times, you need to choose a topic to describe. Your topic can be a person, place, or anything else you can see or touch, taste or smell, hear or imagine.

Make a list of possible topics. In a short description, you cannot say everything there is to say about a topic; so decide in what way you want to describe it. Do you want to describe how your subject looks? Then you would tell about its size, shape, and colors. Do you want to describe how it sounds, or feels, or tastes, or smells? Do you want to tell how your subject moves? In that case, you would use action words like *rushing, jumping,* or *waving.*

List the important *details* about each topic. **Details** are the small parts of a thing. They are the shapes, colors, sounds, smells, and actions of a thing. Details can be phrases or single words.

When you are finished, choose the topic that you have the most to say about. Then add more details.

Selecting Details Read the lists of details below. Decide what each group tells about its topic. Write the letter that matches what the details are describing.

   a. how it looks   **c.** how it feels   **e.** how it moves
   b. how it sounds   **d.** how it smells

__c__ **1.** soft, warm, silky   __e__ **3.** hopping, skipping, jumping

__b__ **2.** loud, blaring, ear-piercing __d__ **4.** fragrant, like perfume, sweet

Writing Details Look at the topics listed below. Then write details for each topic to answer the question. **Details will vary.**

watermelon
How does it taste? _____
_____
_____

mud
How does it feel? _____
_____
_____

a sunset
How does it look? _____
_____
_____

traffic at a busy intersection
How does it sound? _____
_____
_____

Prewriting: Arranging Details

Writing a Description
85

One way to organize your details is in a **natural order.** The order is called *natural* because it is the way you would probably look at these things without even thinking.

Two common natural orders are top-to-bottom order and bottom-to-top order. Tall things, such as mountains or buildings, are often described from bottom to top. People are often described from top to bottom.

Read the following paragraph.

> I looked down at the short, stubby, yellow pencil in my hand. A dull point rested on the paper. The tooth-marked body of the pencil was thick and hard for me to hold. On the top was an orange, worn-out eraser.

The writer first mentions the size and color of the pencil. These are general facts you would notice quickly. She then describes the pencil in bottom-to-top order.

Arranging Details For each topic below, think of four details that tell how the topic looks. Write them on another sheet of paper. Then arrange the details in some order that fits your topic. It may be top-to-bottom, bottom-to-top, front-to-back, left-to-right, inside-to-outside, or some other arrangement. Tell what order you are following. Then write your details in that order. **Orders and details will vary.**

a tree
what order? _____
_____
_____
_____
_____

your classroom
what order? _____
_____
_____
_____
_____

a dog
what order? _____
_____
_____
_____
_____

a sandwich
what order? _____
_____
_____
_____
_____

Writing a Draft

Writing a Description
86

Use your prewriting notes to write a draft of your description. As you write your draft, add details and use exact words to make your description more interesting. Compare these two paragraphs.

> The yard was pretty. It had a big tree with a swing. A flower garden was near the fence. The flowers were petunias and marigolds.

> The back yard was so inviting. In the middle stood a tall, shady elm tree. A wooden rope swing hung from its lowest branch. A flower garden lined the white picket fence. It was full of pink and white petunias and bright orange marigolds.

The first paragraph does not give a clear picture of the yard. The details and exact words in the second paragraph describe the yard more completely.
Follow these guides as you write your draft.

1. **Use adjectives to describe nouns.**
   fence—white picket fence   marigolds—bright orange marigolds

2. **Use exact words to give a clear picture.**
   tree—tall, shady elm tree   was near—lined the white picket fence

3. **Use phrases that add details.**
   swing hung from its lowest branch

Using Details and Exact Words Read the sentence below. Then follow the directions one at a time. Recopy the sentence each time. Notice the difference between your fourth sentence and the original sentence. **Sentences will vary.**

A boy was walking his dog.

1. Add an adjective to describe the boy.
2. Add an adjective to describe the dog.
3. Add a phrase to describe where the boy was walking.
4. Add a word or phrase to describe how he was walking.

_____

_____

_____

Writing Your Draft Begin with an interesting topic sentence that tells what you are describing. Then follow your writing plan as you write your own description. Add details and use exact words as you write.

Revising and Proofreading a Description

Writing a Description
87

When you revise your draft, you try to make your description clearer. Ask yourself these questions as you revise.

Guides for Revising

1. Have I included enough details to give a clear picture of my topic?
2. Should I add adjectives or use more exact words to improve the description?
3. Have I described the actions of my topic?
4. Have I used details that appeal to more than one sense?
5. Are the details in a natural or logical order?

After you revise your paragraph for ideas, proofread it carefully for mistakes in grammar, capitalization, punctuation, and spelling.

Revising a Description The following paragraph does not give a clear description. Use the guides above to revise the paragraph. Add adjectives and phrases to give more details. Describe the actions of the flags. Use exact words. Write your improved paragraph on the lines below. Try to make a clear and interesting picture for the reader. **Revisions will vary.**

The three flags waved in the breeze. They were different colors. could hear them moving. It was a pretty day.

_____
_____
_____
_____
_____

Revising and Proofreading Your Description Revise your own description. Use the guides above. Then proofread your description carefully. Correct errors in grammar, capitalization, punctuation, and spelling. When you have made your description clear and error-free, copy it in your best handwriting. Share it with others.

Review: Writing a Description

Writing a Description
88

Thinking About Descriptions Read the following description. Then answer the questions below.

    The woman in charge of the haunted house had scary hands. Heavy gold bracelets were coiled tightly around each wrist. Her hands had a greenish color. Her long fingers looked like bony daggers. Each fingernail extended far beyond her fingertips. The nails were filed to sharp points. They were painted black. One nail had a small yellow snake head painted on it. The snake's mouth was open and its fangs showed.

1. What is the topic of this description? **a woman's hands**

2. What sense does this description appeal to? **sight**

3. What are two phrases the writer uses to describe shape?
   bony daggers, coiled tightly around, filed to sharp points

4. In what natural order does the writer describe the topic?
   wrists to fingertips

5. What words are used to describe color? **gold bracelets, greenish color, nails painted black, small yellow snake head**

Revising and Proofreading Revise and proofread the following description. Correct errors in grammar, punctuation, capitalization, and spelling. Rewrite the paragraph on the lines below correctly.

    The beuatiful marble egg was polished to a high shine. Light and dark spots of purple mixed to make a deep lavender. The light reflected off the shiney surface. it was a prefect oval It sat on a littel gold circle, With feet.

The beautiful marble egg was polished to a high shine. Light and dark spots of purple mixed to make a deep lavender. The light reflected off the shiny surface. It was a perfect oval. It sat on a little gold circle with feet.

What Are Pronouns?

Understanding Pronouns
89

A pronoun is a word used in place of a noun.

Sara dropped *Sara's* books.   Sara dropped *her* books.

The pronoun *her* is used in place of the noun *Sara*.
Like nouns, pronouns can be singular or plural.

SINGULAR PRONOUNS

Person Speaking:	I	my, mine	me
Person Spoken To:	you	your, yours	you
Person, Place, or Thing Spoken About:	he	his	him
	she	her, hers	her
	it	its	it

PLURAL PRONOUNS

Person Speaking:	we	our, ours	us
Person Spoken To:	you	your, yours	you
Persons, Places, or Things Spoken About:	they	their, theirs	them

Identifying Pronouns Underline the pronoun in each sentence. On the blank, write the noun that the pronoun stands for.

EXAMPLE: Mike rode <u>his</u> bike.   _____Mike_____

1. Sharon picked strawberries. Tammy ate <u>them</u>.   _____strawberries_____
2. Charles, will <u>you</u> answer the question, please?   _____Charles_____
3. Kathy has new skates. <u>She</u> is a good skater.   _____Kathy_____
4. The boys missed the bus. <u>They</u> will be late for school.   _____boys_____
5. The team won <u>its</u> first game.   _____team_____

Using Pronouns for Nouns Write a pronoun to replace the underlined noun.

1. Laura played in <u>Laura's</u> sandbox.   _____her_____
2. Scott tied <u>Scott's</u> shoelaces.   _____his_____
3. José drew a picture. Ray was in <u>the picture</u>.   _____it_____
4. The Scouts wore <u>the Scouts'</u> uniforms.   _____their_____
5. The bird flew to <u>the bird's</u> nest.   _____its_____

Using Pronouns as Subjects

Understanding Pronouns
90

The following pronouns may be used as subjects of sentences.

I   we   you   he   she   it   they

We are going to the beach.   *She* ate lunch.

Be careful with sentences that have two parts in the subject. It may be difficult to choose the correct pronoun. Read the following sentence.

Tanya and (I, me) walked to the library.

To figure out which pronoun to use, try each part separately.

I walked to the library.   Me walked to the library.

Since the pronoun is the subject, use *I*. Use the same pronoun when you put the two parts together.

Tanya and I walked to the library.

These pronouns may **not** be used as the subject:

me   us   him   her   them

Using Pronouns as Subjects Underline the correct subject pronoun.

1. Devon and (she, her) made a snowman.
2. Marisha and (they, them) climbed the mountain.
3. Greg and (me, I) watched television.
4. (We, Us) and the Sullivans had a cookout together.
5. (Him, He) and Rosie are on the track team.
6. Larry and (them, they) are going to the outdoor concert.
7. My mother and (I, me) played tennis this morning.
8. Amy and (we, us) are hungry.
9. (She, Her) and Paul collected old newspapers.
10. Dean's uncle and (him, he) went to the circus.
11. Rima and (her, she) have parts in the school play.
12. Van and (they, them) build model cars.
13. My pen pal and (me, I) write every month.
14. (He, Him) and Gail fixed the loose fence boards.
15. The Bluejays and (we, us) tied for first place.

Using *Me, Us, Her, Him,* and *Them*

Understanding Pronouns
91

● If the pronoun is not the subject of the sentence, you usually use these pronouns:

me   us   her   him   them

Paco waved to *me*.   The bus stopped for *us*.

Use these pronouns in any part of the sentence:

you   it

You helped me.   I helped *you*.

Be careful with sentences like this:

The teacher called on Ken and (me, I).

Decide if the pronoun is the subject. The subject in this sentence is *teacher*. Therefore, the pronoun is not the subject. Choose the correct pronoun, following the rule for *me, us, her, him,* and *them*. The sentence below shows the correct choice.

The teacher called on Ken and me.

Using *Me, Us, Her, Him,* and *Them* Underline the correct pronoun in these sentences.

●
1. The audience applauded for Beth and (they, <u>them</u>).
2. The mail carrier gave letters to Clinton and (he, <u>him</u>).
3. Libby invited Mike and (<u>us</u>, we) to her party.
4. The magician performed a trick for Diana and (<u>us</u>, we).
5. Hail hit Stan and (he, <u>him</u>).
6. Mom bought ice cream cones for Janet and (<u>me</u>, I).
7. The car almost hit Raymond and (she, <u>her</u>).
8. Renee raced past Chuck and (they, <u>them</u>).
9. The dog followed Andy and (<u>me</u>, I) home.
10. Cindy surprised Tina and (she, <u>her</u>).
11. Garrett made a kite for Sarah and (he, <u>him</u>).
12. There were just enough cookies for Lester and (we, <u>us</u>).
13. This table is saved for Jennifer and (<u>them</u>, they).
14. After practice, the coach talked to Paul and (I, <u>me</u>).
15. Adeline's mother took (<u>her</u>, she) and me to the bowling alley.

Using *I* and *Me*, *We* and *Us* Correctly

Understanding Pronouns
92

I* and *Me Whenever you use *I* or *me* with a noun or other pronoun, use *I* or *me* last.

Darren and I collect rocks.   Dad called Nancy and me.
He and I collect rocks.   Dad called her and me.

We and Us When *we* or *us* is used with a noun, it may be hard to choose the right pronoun. Try the sentence without the noun.

(We, Us) joggers run every day.

Say the sentence without the noun *joggers*. Now you can tell that the pronoun is the subject. When the pronoun is the subject part of the sentence, use *we*. The sentence should begin with *We joggers*.

The teacher read a story to (us, we) students.

Try this sentence without the noun *students*. The pronoun is not the subject part of the sentence. When the pronoun is not the subject, use *us*. The sentence should end with *us students*.

Using *I* and *Me*, and *We* and *Us* Choose the correct word or words from the parentheses. Underline them.

1. Kateri took a picture of (<u>Jill and me</u>, me and Jill).
2. (<u>We</u>, Us) girls played basketball.
3. The fire chief talked to (<u>us</u>, we) children.
4. (<u>Warren and I</u>, I and Warren) gave our dog a bath.
5. Ms. Phillips taught the new song to (we, <u>us</u>) singers.
6. Marcy told the secret to (<u>Craig and me</u>, me and Craig).
7. (<u>We</u>, Us) runners entered the race.
8. The water splashed (<u>us</u>, we) swimmers.
9. (<u>Larry and I</u>, I and Larry) are members of the band.
10. (<u>We</u>, Us) fourth-graders have three teachers.
11. The cable car ride was exciting for (we, <u>us</u>) passengers.
12. (<u>We</u>, Us) boys waited in the playground.
13. Please write your autograph for (we, <u>us</u>) fans.
14. The guide took (we, <u>us</u>) riders on the longest trail.
15. (<u>We</u>, Us) students are ready to go home.

Possessive Pronouns

Understanding Pronouns
93

Possessive pronouns are pronouns that show possession. Possessive pronouns do not use any apostrophes.

These are the possessive forms of pronouns:

my, mine	our, ours
your, yours	your, yours
his, her, hers, its	their, theirs

Look at these examples:

This is *my* umbrella.   This umbrella is *mine*.
Those are *your* boots.   Those boots are *yours*.
Colleen is wearing *her* hat. This hat is *hers*.

Using Possessive Pronouns Write a possessive pronoun on the line. Use the information in parentheses.

EXAMPLE: That football is ___theirs___. (The football belongs to them.)

1. That package is ___hers___. (The package belongs to that woman.)

2. This is ___her___ poster. (The poster belongs to the girl.)

3. The lion paced in ___its___ cage. (The cage belongs to the lion.)

4. ___Our___ flowers are blooming. (The flowers belong to us.)

5. ___My___ kitten has soft fur. (The kitten belongs to me.)

6. Jeremy kept ___his___ promise. (The promise belongs to Jeremy.)

7. Brush ___your___ teeth every day. (The teeth belong to you.)

8. The boys played in ___their___ yard. (The yard belongs to the boys.)

9. The winning ticket is ___yours___. (The ticket belongs to you.)

10. This watch is ___mine___. (The watch belongs to me.)

11. Which bus in the lot is ___ours___? (The bus belongs to us.)

12. That house must be ___theirs___. (The house belongs to them.)

13. The large map is ___his___. (The map belongs to the man.)

14. Most animals take good care of ___their___ babies. (The babies belong to the animals.)

15. Girls, which goal is ___yours___? (The goal belongs to the girls.)

Using *Its, Your,* and *Their*

Understanding Pronouns
94

Homophones are words that sound the same or nearly the same, but have different meanings and are spelled differently.

These three sets of homophones involve pronouns. Study their definitions. Notice how they are used in sentences.

its is the possessive form of *it*. *Its* has no apostrophe.
  The bird flew to *its* nest.

it's is the contraction for *it is* or *it has*. *It's* has an apostrophe showing a missing letter or letters.
  It's three o'clock.

your is the possessive form of *you*. *Your* has no apostrophe.
  Your painting is beautiful.

you're is the contraction for *you are*. *You're* has an apostrophe showing a missing letter.
  You're late.

their means belonging to *them*. *Their* has no apostrophe.
  Their dog is a collie.

they're is the contraction for *they are*. *They're* has an apostrophe showing a missing letter.
  They're playing baseball.

there means "at that place."
  The field is over *there*.

Using *Its, Your,* and *Their* Correctly Underline the correct homophone.

1. I found (<u>your</u>, you're) glasses.

2. The cat licked (<u>its</u>, it's) paw.

3. (Their, There, <u>They're</u>) planning to visit the museum.

4. (<u>It's</u>, Its) hard to swim against the current.

5. The Lopezes have wallpapered (<u>their</u>, there, they're) kitchen.

6. (Your, <u>You're</u>) growing as tall as your brother.

7. The plates are kept up (their, <u>there</u>, they're).

8. (<u>Its</u>, It's) claws were long and pointed.

9. Please take care of (<u>your</u>, you're) new clothes.

10. (Its, <u>It's</u>) about time the mail arrived.

Mixed Practice: Understanding Pronouns

Using Pronouns for Nouns Underline the pronoun in each sentence. On the blank, write the noun or nouns that the pronoun stands for.

1. The baby drank <u>her</u> apple juice. _____**baby**_____

2. Don slept late, and <u>he</u> missed the bus. _____**Don**_____

3. Chris, please turn off <u>your</u> radio. _____**Chris**_____

4. Liz and Maria shared <u>their</u> sack lunches. _____**Liz and Maria**_____

5. Dad baked muffins, and Sara ate <u>them</u>. _____**muffins**_____

Using Pronouns Underline the correct pronoun in each sentence.

1. (Him, <u>He</u>) and I collect old coins.

2. Dad took several pictures of Sheila and (<u>me</u>, I).

3. Carol and (<u>we</u>, us) saw the deer.

4. Lorenzo played cards with Gina and (they, <u>them</u>).

5. The thunder frightened our friends and (<u>us</u>, we).

6. (<u>She</u>, Her) and her mother trimmed the lilac hedge.

7. (Them, <u>They</u>) and their parents enjoy sailing.

8. My sister and (me, <u>I</u>) planted strawberries.

9. (Us, <u>We</u>) baton twirlers will lead the parade.

10. Mrs. Holden trained (<u>us</u>, we) singers.

Using Possessive Pronouns Complete each sentence with a possessive pronoun. Use the information in parentheses.

1. John's jacket is in _____**his**_____ room. (The room belongs to John.)

2. Janet feeds _____**her**_____ fish every day. (The fish belong to Janet.)

3. Mary, did you return _____**your**_____ library books today? (The books are Mary's.)

4. Parents should go to _____**their**_____ children's homerooms. (The children belong to the parents.)

5. We are going to sell _____**our**_____ house. (The house belongs to us.)

Using Pronouns in Writing

Understanding Pronouns

Can you describe someone without naming the person? Think of a person in your school. The person can be a student, a teacher, or another school worker. Think up clues to describe your Mystery Person.

Write your Mystery Person clues below. Do not use the person's name. Use only pronouns. Try to use at least five pronouns below in your clues.

Finally, share your clues with a classmate. Have your classmate guess the Mystery Person.

SINGULAR			PLURAL		
I	my, mine	me	we	our, ours	us
you	your, yours	you	you	your, yours	you
he	his	him	they	their, theirs	them
she	her, hers	her			
it	its	it			

Review: Understanding Pronouns

Using Pronouns as Subjects Underline the correct pronoun.

1. Nick and (<u>I</u>, me) played dominoes.
2. Aretha and (<u>she</u>, her) decorated the room.
3. Brad and (us, <u>we</u>) sorted the papers.
4. Lucy and (<u>he</u>, him) live in Oklahoma.
5. (<u>They</u>, Them) and their friends went sledding.

Using *Me, Us, Her, Him,* and *Them* Underline the correct pronoun.

1. The boys threw snowballs at Piper and (<u>us</u>, we).
2. Ms. Bolt gave Betty and (she, <u>her</u>) a ride home.
3. My brother took Adam and (I, <u>me</u>) to the puppet show.
4. Jamie shared lunch with Ted and (he, <u>him</u>).
5. Erik sang a song for (they, <u>them</u>).

Using Possessive Pronouns Write a possessive pronoun on the line. Use the information in the parentheses.

1. Gladys sent _____**her**_____ postcards. (The postcards belong to Gladys.)
2. I cleaned _____**my**_____ room. (The room belongs to me.)
3. What is _____**your**_____ name? (The name belongs to you.)
4. Those pictures are _____**ours**_____. (The pictures belong to us.)
5. The cat drank _____**its**_____ milk. (The milk belongs to the cat.)

Using Pronouns Underline the correct pronoun or phrase.

1. (<u>We</u>, Us) fast growers never have enough clothes.
2. (Therese and I, <u>I and Therese</u>) rode the Blue Streak.
3. My little brother followed (we, <u>us</u>) marchers.
4. The snake has shed (it's, <u>its</u>) skin.
5. We have seen (they're, there, <u>their</u>) vacation pictures.

Fiction Books

Exploring the Library 98

The library has two kinds of books. They are fiction and nonfiction.
Fiction books are stories that a writer made up. The writer of a book is called an **author.**

Fiction books are arranged in alphabetical order. They are arranged according to the first letter of the author's last name. For example, a book by James Daugherty would be put with the *D*'s.

Arranging Fiction Books Look at the first letter of each author's last name. Then write the last names in alphabetical order.

Rachel Field   Henry Winterfeld
Robert Lawson   Barbara Cooney
Fred Gipson   Marcia Brown
Walt Morey   Joseph Krumgold
Mary Norton   Laurence Yep

1. Brown
2. Cooney
3. Field
4. Gipson
5. Krumgold

6. Lawson
7. Morey
8. Norton
9. Winterfeld
10. Yep

Arranging Fiction Books Within a Group Here are two groups of authors' names. The last names within each group begin with the same letter. Number the names according to alphabetical order.

1

- **5** Johanna Spyri
- **1** Ruth Sawyer
- **2** Jackson Scholz
- **3** Maurice Sendak
- **4** Donald J. Sobol
- **6** Mary Stolz

2

- **3** Anne Emery
- **2** Walter D. Edmonds
- **5** Eleanor Estes
- **1** Edward Eager
- **6** Katherine Wigmore Eyre
- **4** Elizabeth Enright

Nonfiction Books

Exploring the Library
99

Nonfiction books are about real persons, places, and things. They are arranged according to their subjects. This means they are arranged in a library according to what they are about.

Nonfiction books are often grouped according to the Dewey Decimal System. This is a system that divides all books into ten categories. Each category includes books on certain subjects. Each category has a different set of numbers.

THE DEWEY DECIMAL SYSTEM

Categories	Subjects	Numbers
General Works	(encyclopedias, atlases)	000–099
Philosophy	(behavior, psychology, philosophy)	100–199
Religion	(the Bible, religion)	200–299
Social Science	(law, education, folklore, government)	300–399
Language	(languages, dictionaries)	400–499
Science	(mathematics, chemistry, animals, plants, astronomy)	500–599
Useful Arts	(gardening, cooking, cars, crafts, television)	600–699
Fine Arts	(music, drawing, acting, games, sports)	700–799
Literature	(poetry, plays, short stories)	800–899
History	(travel, geography, history)	900–999

For example, a book about snakes would be in the Science category. That category has the numbers 500–599. A book about snakes would have a number between 500 and 599. This is the **call number** of the book.

Nonfiction books are arranged in numerical order according to their call numbers. They are arranged in order from 000–999.

Arranging Nonfiction Books Using the Dewey Decimal System, where would you find these books? Write the numbers of the category on the blank.

<u>700–799</u> 1. *What Makes an Orchestra?* by Jan Balet

<u>600–699</u> 2. *Easy Gourmet Cooking* by Bernice Kohn

<u>900–999</u> 3. *The Land and People of Korea* by S. E. Solberg

<u>800–899</u> 4. *Rhymes About Us* by Marchette Chute

<u>700–799</u> 5. *Drawing People* by Elliott Ivenbaum

<u>300–399</u> 6. *State and Local Governments* by Laurence Santrey

<u>200–299</u> 7. *Bible Stories* by William Anthony

<u>000–099</u> 8. *Rand McNally Road Atlas*

<u>000–099</u> 9. *Compton's Encyclopedia*

<u>500–599</u> 10. *Unusual Aquarium Fishes* by Alan Mark Fletcher

Using the Card Catalog

Exploring the Library
100

The card catalog has information on every book in the library. The information is on cards arranged alphabetically. Each card has a call number in the upper left-hand corner.

The card catalog has three cards for every book. They are the **author card,** the **title card,** and the **subject card.** Each card has the same information, but it is arranged in different ways.

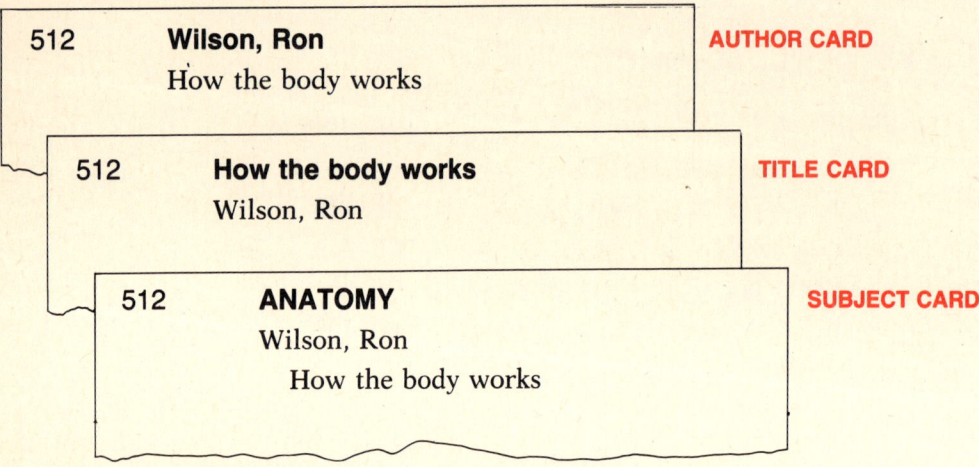

1. The **author card** gives the author's name, last name first, on the top line. The card is filed according to the last name.
2. The **title card** gives the title of the book on the first line. The card is filed according to the first important word of the title.
3. The **subject card** gives the subject name on the top line. The card is filed according to the subject name.

Understanding the Card Catalog Decide which catalog card you will need in the following situations. Write **author card, title card,** or **subject card** on the line.

1. You want a book on collies.   <u>subject card</u>

2. You want a book by Kenneth Grahame.   <u>author card</u>

3. You are looking for the book *The Borrowers*.   <u>title card</u>

Using the Card Catalog Choose two of these subjects. Use the card catalog to find one book on each subject. List the titles, authors, and call numbers of these books on a separate sheet of paper. **Books will vary.**

1. Canada
2. Christopher Columbus
3. Baseball
4. Telescopes

Using Special Parts of a Book

Exploring the Library
101

Books can give you the information you need about a subject. To find out if a book has information about a certain topic, you can look in two places, the **table of contents** and the **index.**

The **table of contents** is found at the beginning of a book. Almost all nonfiction and some fiction books have a table of contents. The table of contents lists every chapter in the book and the page on which the chapter begins. By looking in the table of contents, you can find out if a book contains a whole chapter about your topic.

An **index** is found at the back of almost every nonfiction book. It is a list of topics that are discussed in the book. The topics are listed in alphabetical order. Each topic, or entry, is followed by the numbers of the pages on which that topic is discussed.

Here is an example of an index entry:

comets, 82–86

This entry tells you that comets are discussed on pages 82 to 86.

If you are reading a book and come across a word you do not understand, you can look up the word in the **glossary** of the book. A glossary is found at the back of many nonfiction books before the index. It is a list of the difficult words from the book, along with their definitions. The words are listed in alphabetical order.

Finding Information in Books Fill in the chart below. The first block has been done for you.

	What is it?	What kind of book do you find it in?	Where is it placed in the book?
Table of Contents	A list of every chapter in the book and the page on which the chapter begins	Almost all nonfiction, some fiction	Beginning of book
Index	A list of the topics in the book, in alphabetical order, followed by page numbers	Almost every nonfiction book	At back of book
Glossary	A list of difficult words from the book, with definitions	Many nonfiction books	At back of book before index

Using an Encyclopedia

Exploring the Library
102

Encyclopedias are **reference books.** They contain thousands of articles. The articles are in alphabetical order. Some are about subjects. They are arranged according to the first letter of the subject name. Other articles are about people. They are alphabetized according to the first letter of the person's last name.

Each book in a set of encyclopedias is called a **volume.** On the back of each volume are letters or words. They tell you what part of the alphabet is covered in that volume.

Finding the Right Volume Choose a set of encyclopedias. Find the volume that has the article on each of the topics below. Write the letter, letters, or words that are on the backs of the volumes.

Answers will vary according to encyclopedias used.

1. Coast Guard _____

2. Belgium _____

3. Heart _____

4. Robot _____

5. Guinea pig _____

6. Babe Ruth _____

7. Iron _____

8. Yellowstone National Park _____

9. Photography _____

10. Beverly Sills _____

11. Ohio _____

12. Pyramids _____

13. Robert E. Lee _____

14. Anteaters _____

15. Zithers _____

Review: Exploring the Library

Finding Books and Information Complete these sentences.

1. Fiction books are arranged in ____alphabetical____ order.

2. Nonfiction books are arranged in ____numerical *or* number____ order by subjects.

3. The index of a book is found in the ____back____ of the book.

4. The ____table of contents____ lists every chapter of a book.

5. To find an encyclopedia entry about a person, look up the person's ____last____ name.

Arranging Fiction Books Look at the first letter of each author's last name. Then write the last names in alphabetical order.

Jean Merrill
Robert Newman
Isabelle Holland
Mirra Ginsburg
Hadley Irwin

1. ____Ginsburg____
2. ____Holland____
3. ____Irwin____
4. ____Merrill____
5. ____Newman____

Using the Card Catalog Decide which catalog card you will use in the following situations. Write **author card, title card,** or **subject card** on the lines. Then write the letter you would look under.

1. You want a book by Lois Lenski.

   ____author card   L____

2. You want a book on Holland.

   ____subject card   H____

3. You are looking for the book *Chicken Soup with Rice.*

   ____title card   C____

4. You are looking for a book about how television works.

   ____subject card   T____

5. You want a book by Rudyard Kipling.

   ____author card   K____

Thinking About Writing To Tell How

Writing To Tell How
104

Sometimes you write to explain how to do or make something. Start by clearly stating what you are explaining. Then list the equipment the reader will need, if any. Finally, tell all of the steps the reader will need to follow. Explain the steps clearly and in the right order.

Look at the following paragraphs that tell how to make something.

> You can make an unusual and beautiful three-dimensional picture from simple materials. You will need several different shapes of pasta, such as elbow or shell macaroni, spaghetti, and rotini. Try to gather unusual shapes. In addition, you will need a piece of white paper, a pencil, glue, and gold spray paint.
>
> First, sketch a design on the paper. Then arrange the different shapes of uncooked pasta to fill in the sketch. When you are satisfied with your arrangement, glue the pieces of pasta onto the paper. Let the glue dry. Then spray paint the whole paper, including the pasta, with gold paint. When it has dried, your creation will look like a gold sculpture.

Studying Paragraphs That Tell How Reread the paragraphs above. Then answer the following questions.

1. What is the main idea of these paragraphs?
   how to make a three-dimensional picture

2. In which sentence is the main idea stated? *first sentence*

3. What equipment is needed to follow the instructions? *different shapes of uncooked pasta, white paper, pencil, glue, gold spray paint*

4. Five steps are given for making the picture. List the steps in the order they were given.
   1. *sketch a design on the paper*
   2. *arrange pasta to fill in sketch*
   3. *glue pasta to paper*
   4. *let glue dry*
   5. *spray paint the picture with gold paint*

5. Could the order of the steps be changed? *no*

Prewriting: Planning To Tell How

Writing To Tell How
105

Your first step in writing a paragraph that tells how is to decide exactly what you will explain. Choose a topic that you know well. Think of what you can do or make that someone else might want to learn. You might choose to write about a subject that you want to learn more about. For more topic ideas, look through some books in the Useful Arts section of the library. These books are numbered between 600 and 699.

It is important to organize your ideas when you plan to tell how. Write your topic at the top of a paper. Then make notes about the steps. List all the supplies needed. Next, list all the remaining steps of the process. Number the steps in the order they should be done.

Recognizing Step-by-Step Order Look at the prewriting notes below. The steps are out of order. Number the steps in a clear, logical order.

TOPIC: How To Play Clothing Relay Race
SUPPLIES: two equal piles of adult clothes, including mittens or gloves, socks, shoes, pants, shirts, and hats

Steps:

__3__ Race begins as first person from each team runs to team's pile and puts all clothing on.

__2__ Each team lines up a good distance away from its pile.

__5__ First player runs back to second team member, who runs and dresses.

__1__ Before the race, players are divided into two teams.

__4__ That player takes the clothing off and puts it back into pile.

__6__ First team whose members have all dressed and undressed wins.

Prewriting: Planning Your Paragraph Choose a project that you can explain how to make or do. Write your topic at the top of your paper. List the equipment needed. Then list the steps to be followed. Be sure the steps are in the right order.

Writing a Draft

Writing To Tell How
106

Begin your draft with a topic sentence that tells what you are explaining. Try to make this sentence clear and interesting. Then turn the steps from your writing plan into complete sentences.

As you write, use signal words to make your directions easy to follow. These are words like *first, second, next, then, while, now,* and *finally.* They are signals to the reader that you are beginning new steps.

Using Signal Words Copy the paragraph below and add signal words. Add words such as *first, next, then, now,* and *finally* where you think they will help the reader most. **Position and choice of signal words may vary. Possible answer is suggested below.**

Follow these steps to wash clothes in a washing machine. Divide the dirty clothing into piles of dark and light colors. Set the machine dial for warm water. Measure the detergent according to the directions on the detergent box or bottle. Loosely load the clothing into the machine. Pour in the detergent, and start the washing machine cycle. Close the lid, and let the machine do the rest!

Follow these steps to wash clothes in a washing machine. First, divide the dirty clothing into piles of dark and light colors. Next, set the machine dial for warm water. Then, measure the detergent according to the directions on the detergent box or bottle. Now, loosely load the clothing into the machine. Pour in the detergent, and start the washing machine cycle. Finally, close the lid, and let the machine do the rest!

Writing Your Draft Use your prewriting notes to write a draft of your paragraph. Start with an interesting topic sentence that tells what you are explaining. Make sentences from your step-by-step instructions. Add signal words to help show the order.

Revising and Proofreading a Draft

Writing To Tell How

Revise your paragraph to make your directions clear. As you revise, ask yourself these questions.

1. Are the directions easy to understand?
2. Have I included all the equipment needed?
3. Have I explained every step in the right order?
4. Have I added signal words to make the order clear?
5. Do I need to add any ideas to make the instructions clearer?

When you finish revising, ask a friend to read your paragraph and follow your instructions. Use your friend's suggestions for further revising.

Next, proofread your draft. As you proofread, add a comma after any signal words such as *first* or *finally* if they come first in the sentence. Correct mistakes in grammar, capitalization, punctuation, and spelling. Then copy your paragraph in your best handwriting. You might add pictures or sketches to help the reader understand the directions.

Proofreading Proofread the following paragraph. Mark the mistakes with proofreading symbols. Then rewrite the paragraph on your own paper. **See answer below.**

¶ Amuse a younger brother or sister with a puppet show. All you need is a paper bag, crayons or markers, glue, crumpled paper, and string. First Draw or paint a face and body on the bag. Decorate the body part of the bag with construction paper and yarn. Make wholes in the sides of the bag for your fingers your fingers will be the arms of the puppet. Stuff the head with crumpled paper. Tie a string or yarn tightly around the neck. Now your ready too preform.

Revising and Proofreading Your Draft Revise your own draft, using the questions above. Have a friend try your directions and make suggestions for improvements. Then proofread your paragraph and correct all the errors you find. Copy your corrected paragraph neatly. Add pictures to illustrate your directions if possible.

Amuse a younger brother or sister with a puppet show. All you need is a paper bag, crayons or markers, glue, crumpled paper, and string. First, draw or paint a face and body on the bag. Decorate the body part of the bag with construction paper and yarn. Make holes in the sides of the bag for your fingers. Your fingers will be the arms of the puppet. Stuff the head with crumpled paper. Tie a string or yarn tightly around the neck. Now you're ready to perform.

Review: Writing To Tell How

Writing To Tell How 108

Thinking About Writing To Tell How Read this paragraph. Then answer the questions below.

It is fun to make a booklet of favorite family recipes. Gather note cards, a hole punch, construction paper, a piece of yarn, a pen, and crayons or markers. First, copy on note cards the recipes your family especially likes. Next, glue each note card on a separate piece of construction paper. Under each recipe card, draw a picture of the dish it makes. When the pages are complete, gather them together. Add a blank page for a cover. Then, punch holes in the left-hand corners of the pages. Thread yarn through the holes, and tie the pages together to make a booklet. Finally, decorate the cover page with pictures of food, and write the name of your family in large letters. You have created a family treasure which can be used by all!

1. What is the main idea of this paragraph? **how to make a family recipe booklet**

2. What supplies are needed? **note cards, a hole punch, construction paper, a piece of yarn, a pen, crayons or markers**

3. What is the last step in the directions? **decorate the cover page with pictures of food and the family's name**

4. What signal words were used in the paragraph? **First, Next, Then, Finally**

5. Could you change the order of the steps and still make the booklet? **yes**

Revising Read the following set of directions. In the spaces above the lines, add signal words to help show the order of the steps. Then add a sentence to finish the paragraph. **Signal words and ending sentences will vary.**

Anyone can make a long distance call by direct dialing. Dial 1. This signals that the call is long distance. Dial the area code. This is the three-digit number that sends the call to the right area of the country. Dial the seven-digit number of the person you are calling.

Making Announcements

Improving Speaking and Listening Skills

An **announcement** is a short speech that tells the listeners about something that is going to happen. It gives important details about the event. A good announcement includes all the important facts: **who, what, when,** and **where.**

You should prepare your announcement carefully. Gather and arrange your facts. Make sure your information is correct. Practice making your announcement. Speak slowly and clearly. Make sure you are loud enough to be heard.

Arranging the Facts Number the following facts in the order you think they should be announced. **Order may vary slightly.**

__4__ A $15.00 donation will be required for any pet adopted.

__3__ Interested persons should come to the entertainment area on Tuesday, February 6, between 10 A.M. and 2 P.M.

__1__ The Humane Society will sponsor "Adopt-a-Pet Day" at the shopping mall next week.

__2__ At that time, dogs and cats will be available for adoption.

__5__ Don't miss this event if you have been thinking about adding a pet to your family.

Checking for Important Details Read the following announcement. Decide what information has been left out. Write a sentence giving the missing detail.

Marge and David Wolf are planning a get-acquainted brunch for old and new members of the Pioneer School Band. The brunch will be held on Friday, September 12, at 11:30 A.M. Band members are asked to bring their membership cards for admission. Uniforms are not required.

Sentences will vary but should include where the brunch will be held.

Using the Telephone

Improving Speaking and Listening Skills

The telephone is a convenient way to communicate with one another. Telephone messages are important to both the caller and the person who is to receive the message. Remember these tips for using the telephone.

- Be polite on the telephone.
- Speak clearly and give your name.
- Plan what you want to say before calling someone.
- If you need to take a message, write it down.
- Read back the message to check the facts.
- Say goodbye politely.

To be safe, never tell a caller that you are home alone. Simply say that your parent cannot come to the phone at this time, and offer to take a message. Write down what the caller says. Then read back what you have written to be sure it is correct.

Taking Telephone Messages Decide which of the following pieces of information are probably not important to include in your written telephone message. Cross them out.

At 5:00, Dad called from his office. He said he'll be a little late for dinner. He needs to drop Mr. Perry off at the train station. ~~I was drying my hair when he called.~~ He said to go ahead and start dinner without him. He'll be home by 6 for sure. ~~It sounded like there were telephones ringing in the background. I think I heard Mr. Perry's voice. I'll bet his car broke down again.~~

Leaving Telephone Messages Imagine that you have just returned home from playing at a friend's house. You suddenly realize that you left an important book in your friend's room. When you call the friend to ask him or her to bring it to school tomorrow, your friend's mother answers. Ask her to take a message instead. Write the message you want her to give your friend. Try acting this out with a partner after you prepare the message.

Messages will vary.

_____
_____
_____
_____

Understanding Fact and Opinion

Learning To Think Clearly

An opinion is one person's idea about someone or something. Here are two opinions:

> That book is exciting.

> That book is boring.

These opinions are opposites. They are neither right nor wrong. A person would have to explain his or her reasons for thinking a certain way.

A fact is true. It can be proved. Here are two facts:

> That book is about space travel.

> That book has a red cover.

Each fact is true. It does not have to be explained.

Understanding Fact and Opinion Five of these sentences are opinions. Five are facts. Write **opinion** on the line before the sentences that are opinions. Write **fact** on the line before the sentences that are facts.

___opinion___ 1. Jumping on a pogo stick is fun.

___opinion___ 2. This bread smells delicious.

___fact___ 3. Baby bears are called cubs.

___opinion___ 4. Fall is the most beautiful season of the year.

___fact___ 5. The Grand Canyon is in Arizona.

___fact___ 6. Hail is made of ice particles.

___opinion___ 7. My dog is the smartest dog in the world.

___fact___ 8. John Adams was our second President.

___fact___ 9. Giraffes eat leaves from tall trees.

___opinion___ 10. That joke was not funny.

Forming Opinions Write a one-sentence opinion about one of these topics.

    rainy days   peanut butter sandwiches   baseball   roller coasters

___Opinions will vary.___

Understanding Generalizations

Learning To Think Clearly
112

Generalizations are statements about a whole group of people, objects, or actions. Generalizations are not always true. They might not be true for every member of a group, or they might not be true all the time. Read this generalization:

> Everybody likes hot dogs.

Some people do not like hot dogs. The generalization is untrue. *Many people like hot dogs* is a true generalization.

Statements containing these words may be too general to be true.

everybody	nobody	never	all the time
everything	all	always	every

Statements that contain words like *most, sometimes, often,* or *usually* can more often be believed. Whenever you come across a generalization, pay careful attention to the words. Decide whether the generalization is too broad to be true.

Understanding Generalizations In the blank next to each statement, write **T** if the generalization is true. Write **U** if it is untrue.

1. All poodles are dogs. __T__

2. All people love dogs. __U__

3. Many garages are not very clean. __T__

4. Girls are always shorter than boys the same age. __U__

5. The sun never shines on February 2, Groundhog Day. __U__

6. Babies always love car rides. __U__

7. This magic trick will fool everyone. __U__

8. Many squirrels have homes in hollow trees. __T__

9. Some animals live in very cold places. __T__

10. People living in hot countries usually wear light clothing. __T__

Avoiding Generalizations Read these untrue generalizations. Underline the word or words that make each untrue. Then rewrite each generalization to make it true.

Rewritten statements will vary.

1. <u>Everyone</u> loves reading about magic.

_____

2. <u>Nobody</u> is interested in the habits of goldfish.

_____

Understanding Slanted Language

Words can create feelings. You could trust a *respectable person,* but you could not trust a *slick character.* Language that creates feelings is called **slanted language.**

Here are three synonyms: *dull, uneventful,* and *peaceful. Peaceful* suggests a good feeling. We call it a **positive** word. *Dull* suggests an unpleasant feeling. We call it a **negative** word. *Uneventful* does not suggest any particular feeling. We call it a **neutral** word.

Recognizing Slanted Language Decide whether each sentence below expresses a positive feeling or a negative feeling. Write *P* next to the sentences that express a positive feeling and *N* next to those that express a negative feeling. Then underline two words from each sentence that help create that feeling.

1. The <u>eerie</u> ship <u>creaked</u> and <u>groaned</u> in the wind. __**N**__

2. Our apartment is <u>clean</u> and <u>spacious</u>. __**P**__

3. The panda curled into a <u>cute</u>, <u>furry</u> ball. __**P**__

4. That lobster has <u>nasty</u> claws and four <u>creepy</u> feelers. __**N**__

5. Get that <u>slimy</u>, <u>smelly</u> frog away from me! __**N**__

6. The frog is a <u>wonderful</u> jumper and a <u>skillful</u> hunter. __**P**__

7. That <u>flimsy</u> jacket is <u>moth-eaten</u> and <u>faded</u>. __**N**__

8. The <u>sweet</u> juice of the peach <u>refreshed</u> her. __**P**__

9. The <u>dark</u> forest <u>screamed</u> with <u>danger</u>. __**N**__

10. Sunshine <u>sparkled</u> on the <u>babbling</u> brook. __**P**__

Review: Learning To Think Clearly

Understanding Fact and Opinion Decide whether each statement is fact or opinion. Write **F** if the sentence states a fact. Write **O** if the sentence states an opinion.

__F__ 1. A wheel with teeth is called a *gear*.

__O__ 2. Drawing pictures of people is easy.

__O__ 3. The best cheese comes from the Netherlands.

__F__ 4. A number with one hundred zeros is called a *googol*.

__F__ 5. Starch is used to make clothing stiffer.

Understanding Generalizations Decide whether each generalization is true or untrue. Write **T** if the generalization is true. Write **U** if it is untrue. Underline the word or words that make statements untrue.

__U__ 1. Children ought to eat soybeans <u>all the time</u>.

__T__ 2. Few people can speak four languages.

__T__ 3. Mayors often take part in holiday parades.

__U__ 4. <u>Nobody</u> eats hot dogs for breakfast.

__U__ 5. Animals are <u>always</u> raised by their mothers.

Understanding Slanted Language Decide whether each phrase expresses a positive or negative feeling. On the blank next to each statement, write **P** for positive or **N** for negative.

__P__ 1. colorful, exotic bird

__N__ 2. sticky, humid weather

__N__ 3. cold, greasy leftovers

__P__ 4. sparkling, clean dishes

__P__ 5. comfortable, sturdy clothes

Thinking About Opinions

Writing To Explain an Opinion
115

The way you think or feel about something is your **opinion.** When you explain your opinion to others, either in speaking or in writing, you should give reasons why you think the way you do.

People may have different opinions about the same thing. For example, your mother might say,

> I really enjoy picnics. The fresh air seems to make the food taste better. The smell of the grass and the breeze in my hair make me feel ten years old again!

Your grandmother, however, might express an opposite opinion.

> I don't enjoy picnics at all. I can't stand the thought of bugs in my food. There aren't any comfortable chairs at picnics. I always go home with a sore back and sand in my shoes.

As you can see, opinions are not right or wrong. They are just the way people feel about things.

Thinking About Opinions Answer the following questions about the two opinions expressed above.

1. What is the mother's opinion of picnics? **She enjoys them.**

2. What are the mother's reasons for feeling that way?

   Fresh air makes food taste better; being outdoors makes her feel young.

3. What is the grandmother's opinion of picnics?

   She does not enjoy them.

4. What are the grandmother's reasons for feeling that way?

   She doesn't like bugs in her food; there are no comfortable chairs; she gets a sore back and sandy shoes.

Prewriting: Planning a Paragraph

Writing To Explain an Opinion

Writing to share your opinion, like other writing, needs planning. Planning helps you explain your opinion clearly. Here are some suggestions to help you.

1. **Think of an opinion.** If your topic is not assigned, make a list of things you might wish to write about. Talk with others, or look through the newspaper. Think of people or events about which you have strong feelings. Then select a topic from your list.

2. **Decide on a main idea.** Narrow your topic to a single idea that you care about. Write your opinion in one sentence. Use words that express your feelings as clearly as possible.

3. **List your reasons.** Write as many reasons as you can think of for your opinion. Some reasons may be your own. Others may come from books, magazines, or other people.

4. **Make a writing plan.** Write your main idea. Then arrange your reasons in the order you want to present them. You will want to save your most convincing reason for the end of the paragraph.

Listing Reasons Read the following opinion. Decide whether you agree or disagree with it. Then write two reasons that support the opinion, or two reasons that go against the opinion. **Opinions and reasons will vary.**

Opinion: Students should have gym class every day.

I agree. _____   I disagree. _____

Reasons: _____

_____

_____

Prewriting: Planning Your Paragraph Choose an opinion you feel strongly about. Decide what you want to say about it. List reasons why you feel as you do. Arrange your reasons in a writing plan.

Writing a Draft

Writing To Explain an Opinion

To begin your draft, state your opinion clearly as a topic sentence. Avoid words like *everybody, always, never,* and *the best* or *the worst*. These words can make your sentence too broad to be believed. Also, avoid words like *I think* or *I feel*. These words are not needed to identify your statement as an opinion.

After you write your topic sentence, write your reasons in sentence form. Follow your writing plan, and put your most important reason last. Use signal words such as *first, second, also,* and *most important* to help your readers see how you rank your reasons.

Stating Your Opinion Clearly Compare homemade food to food from a fast food restaurant. Think about which is better for you, which tastes better, which is more convenient. Express an opinion about which you prefer. Write a topic sentence that states your opinion clearly.   **Opinions and sentences will vary.**

Opinion: _____

_____

Topic Sentence: _____

_____

Writing Your Draft Use your own prewriting notes to write your draft. State your opinion clearly in the topic sentence. Write your reasons in full sentences, according to your writing plan. Add signal words where they will help.

_____
_____
_____
_____
_____
_____
_____
_____
_____

Revising and Proofreading

Writing To Explain an Opinion

118

As you revise, first make sure that your opinion is stated clearly. Next, be certain that all of your reasons support your opinion. Have you given enough reasons? Leave out weak or unimportant reasons. You might add examples to help the reader understand your reasons. Finally, some paragraphs need an ending sentence to "wrap up" the main idea. If yours does, you will want to add it here.

After you revise your paragraph, proofread it for mistakes in grammar, capitalization, punctuation, and spelling.

Revising a Paragraph Revise and proofread the paragraph below. Use the following directions to help you. Mark your corrections on the paragraph, using proofreading marks. **Answers will vary. Suggested answers are given.**

1. In sentence 1, take out the unnecessary words *I think*. Capitalize *all*.

2. In sentence 2, add a word or phrase to signal the first reason.

3. In sentence 3, correct the form of an adjective used to compare.

4. In sentence 4, correct two misspelled words.

5. Add a final reason or a sentence to wrap up the paragraph at the end.

¹~~I think~~ all school weeks should be four days instead of five. **First of all,** ²Students would be less tired after a three-day weekend. ³They could work ~~more~~ harder on the four days. ⁴Even teachers ~~woud~~ **would** be fresher and more ~~exited~~ **excited** about teaching. ⁵On three-day weekends, everyone has more time to travel. **Last sentences will vary.** _____

_____

_____

Revising and Proofreading Your Draft Read your own draft carefully and think of ways to improve it. Make your opinion and reasons as clear and convincing as you can. Proofread your paragraph and correct mistakes. Finally, recopy your paragraph and share it with others.

Review: Writing To Explain an Opinion

Stating Opinions Rewrite the following opinions to make good topic sentences. Change words when necessary to state the opinions more clearly and avoid generalizations.

EXAMPLE
Opinion: Everybody in the whole world ought to swim because they will be safe and they'll get exercise and they'll like it.

Revised: For safety, exercise, and fun, swimming is a great sport.   **Sentences will vary.**

1. Our school lunches are the pits.

2. There should be a national holiday or something for kids.

3. All people in dangerous jobs should be paid lots of money.

4. Dogs have got to be the smartest animals in the world.

5. It's not fair that there's no girls' baseball team at our park.

Thinking About Reasons Read the following opinion and set of reasons. Put a check next to the two reasons that do **not** support the opinion well. Then add one more reason of your own that would support the opinion.

Opinion: Jeff Baker will make an excellent Student Council president.

Reasons:

✓ He is my very best friend, and a great pitcher.

____ He is friendly, outgoing, and gets along with classmates.

✓ Jeff's mother knows Mrs. Chandler, the principal.

____ He knows our school's problems and has some good ideas about how to correct them.

____ Other students respect him and sees him as a leader.

Reasons will vary.

Learning Skills for Better Reading

Sharpening Study Skills
120

You read for many different reasons. The way you read depends on your purpose. To study, you need to read slowly and carefully. You must read every word.

Sometimes you need to read quickly to find out what a book contains, or to find a piece of information. This type of fast reading is called **skimming.**

To skim a page, move your eyes quickly over the whole page. Look at headings, words in large or heavy type, words in color, and pictures or charts. In this way you can get an overview of the page. You do not need to read every word to find out what the page is about. To get an overview of a whole book, skim the table of contents.

Sometimes you need to find one particular fact. You can skim a page to find that fact. Glance at headings and look for key words to help you find what you want. Do not read every word.

Skimming Read and answer each question below.

1. Skim the following list of summer classes at a camp.

    What time is the class in printmaking? __11:00__

Drawing I	9:00	Calligraphy I	10:00
Collage	9:00	Printmaking	11:00
Clay Things	10:00	Watercolors	11:00
Drawing II	10:00	Calligraphy II	11:00

2. Look at the table of contents for this book. If your teacher planned to spend one week on each chapter, how many weeks would be needed to complete the book? __24__

3. Skim the following list, which gives the fastest speeds of many animals. Are the two fastest animals to be found on land, in the water, or in the air? __in the air__

LAND (miles per hour)	WATER (mph)	AIR (mph)
Turtle—.1 mph	Goldfish—4 mph	Robin—30 mph
Snake—2 mph	Trout—5 mph	Owl—40 mph
Elephant—20 mph	Whale—20 mph	Dragonfly—50 mph
House Cat—30 mph	Dolphin—25 mph	Hummingbird—60 mph
Greyhound—40 mph	Barracuda—30 mph	Canvasback Duck—70 mph
Gazelle—50 mph	Sailfish—30 mph	Golden Eagle—120 mph
Cheetah—70 mph		Duck Hawk—180 mph

    (from *The World Book Encyclopedia*)

Taking Notes from a Book

Sharpening Study Skills
121

Sometimes you read to collect facts about a subject. Taking notes is a good way to remember the information you find.

Write your notes on 3″ × 5″ index cards. At the top of each, write the title and author of the book where you got the information. Then write a fact about your subject. Write the fact in your own words. Write each fact on a separate card.

The following paragraph is from the book *The World of Plants* by Carol McGraw. Below it is an example of a note card.

> Have you ever heard of plants that eat insects? That may sound strange, but there are some plants that do catch and eat insects. One of these plants is the Venus's flytrap.

The World of Plants — **Title**
by Carol McGraw — **Author**
The Venus's flytrap is a plant that catches and eats insects. — **Fact**

Taking Notes Read this paragraph from the book *Indians of the Plains* by Donald Thomas. In the space below, write the title of the book and the author. Then write one fact you learned. Write it in your own words.

> The Plains Indians lived in tepees. Tepees were homes that looked like big tents. They were made of poles covered with buffalo skins. The Indians could take down their tepees quickly when they wanted to move.

Indians of the Plains
by Donald Thomas

Fact will vary.

Taking Notes from an Encyclopedia

Sharpening Study Skills
122

You will be finding information about your subject in library books. You will also be reading about it in encyclopedias. The notes you take should list the name of the encyclopedia at the top. Next, write the name of the article where you found the information. Then write a fact about your subject in your own words.

Here is an example of a note showing a fact from an encyclopedia.

The World Book Encyclopedia	**Encyclopedia**
"Venus's Flytrap"	**Article**
The leaves of a Venus's flytrap act like a trap.	**Fact**

Taking Notes from an Encyclopedia Article The following is an article from *The World Book Encyclopedia*. Below are the outlines of two note cards. On each card write the name of the encyclopedia, the name of the article, and one fact you learned. Write the fact in your own words.

TOTEM, *TOH tuhm,* is a symbol for a tribe, clan, family, or a person. The Chippewa, or Ojibwa, Indians first used the term for the animals or birds associated with their clans. The clan totem may be a bird, fish, animal, plant, or other natural object. Some groups consider the totem as an ancestor of the clan. A clan may have rules against killing or eating the species to which the totem belongs. Clan members are often known by the name of the totem. Some clans consider the totem holy and pray to it. Totemism, as a form of religion, may have been widespread among tribal peoples.

Many American Indian tribes, particularly those of the Pacific Northwest, carved the family and clan emblems on totem poles. The tribe held a *potlatch,* or feast, when the totem poles were put up.

Totem poles may be seen in Vancouver and Victoria, B.C.; Seattle, Wash.; in the Field Museum of Natural History and in Lincoln Park in Chicago; and in the American Museum of Natural History in New York.   FRED EGGAN

The World Book Encyclopedia
"Totem"
Fact will vary.

The World Book Encyclopedia
"Totem"
Fact will vary.

Taking Tests

Sharpening Study Skills
123

You take tests to show you and your teacher how much you have learned. When you are going to take a test, remember these tips:

1. Be prepared. Get plenty of sleep the night before, and eat a good breakfast. Bring all the materials you need for the test with you, such as pencils, paper, a ruler, and so on.

2. Understand the directions. Read or listen carefully to directions. Ask questions if you do not understand them.

3. Think about what each question asks. Then select the best answer. Mark your answer according to the directions.

When you take a test, you will first be asked to give information about yourself. On many tests, you will be writing this information in rows of little boxes called **grids.**

This is an example of a grid. A boy named Nicholas Rosenthal has filled it out. As you read the rules below the grid, notice how Nicholas followed them when he filled in his name.

NAME

| R | O | S | E | N | T | H | A | L | | N | I | C | H | O |

1. Print neatly. Do not write in cursive.
2. Start in the first box.
3. Fill in your last name first. Print your complete last name.
4. Skip a space between words.
5. Fill in as much of your first name as you can. Do not try to squeeze letters in at the end of the grid.

Another way of giving information is to fill in circles or squares. Look at these examples.

● boy   0 girl   Grade   0 3   ● 4   0 5

Giving Information About Yourself Fill in the grids and circles below, giving information about yourself. Remember to follow the rules listed above.
Information will vary.

NAME

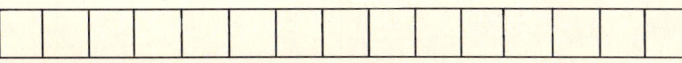

SCHOOL

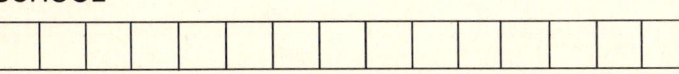

0 boy   0 girl   Grade   0 3   0 4   0 5

Answering Test Questions

Sharpening Study Skills
124

The directions on a test will tell you how and where to mark your answers. Follow the rules below when you are marking your answers to test questions.

1. Mark your answers exactly the way the directions tell you to.
2. Mark only one answer for each question.
3. If you are marking your answers on a special answer sheet, be sure to match the number of the question with the number on the answer sheet.
4. If you are marking your answers in circles, be sure to darken the circles completely and neatly. Do not write in the circles.
5. If you want to change an answer, erase your mark completely and carefully. Do not tear the paper.

Marking Your Answers Study these four test questions and answers. If the student made a mistake in marking the answer, write what he or she did wrong on the lines below. If there is nothing wrong, write **Correct**.

TEST PAPER

Directions: Choose the correct answer and fill in the circle on the answer sheet. Do not write on this paper.

1. Another word for *correct* is
   A. right   B. wrong   C. simple
2. Another word for *hurry* is
   A. slow   B. jump   C. rush
3. The opposite of *bright* is
   A. shiny   B. dark   C. smooth
4. The opposite of *chilly* is
   A. warm   B. cool   C. soft

ANSWER SHEET

1. A● B○ C○
2. A● B○ C●
3. A○ B⊠ C○
4. A○ B○ C○

1. _Correct_

2. _Two answers given_

3. _Letter crossed out; circle not darkened_

4. _No answer given_

Review: Sharpening Study Skills

Skimming Skim the table of contents of this book to answer the following questions.

1. How many pages are in the chapter about adverbs? __6__

2. How many practice pages are in the **Irregular Verbs** section? __10__

3. What is the fourth chapter called? __Understanding Verbs__

4. Which page starts the chapter on narrative writing? __56__

5. What page reviews **Exploring the Library?** __103__

Taking Notes Suppose you are taking notes from an encyclopedia article. Answer the questions below.

1. What do you write your notes on? __note cards__

2. What two things should you write at the top of the card?

   __name of the encyclopedia, name of the article__

3. How many facts should be written on the card? __one__

4. Why do you take notes? __to remember information__

Marking Test Answers Look at the questions and answers from one student's test below. Circle the number of the question that is answered correctly according to the directions.

TEST PAPER

Directions: Choose the correct answer and fill in the circle on the answer sheet. Do not write on the test paper.

1. The boys _____ to school.
   A. walk   B. walks   C. walking
2. The alarm clock _____ .
   A. ring   B. rings   C. ringing
3. The robin *flies* to her nest.
   A. fly   B. flies   C. flying
4. The tulips are _____ .
   A. bloom   B. blooms   C. blooming

ANSWER SHEET

(1.)	A ●	B 0	C 0
2.	A 0	B ●	C ●
3.	A 0	B 0	C 0
4.	A 0	B 0	C ✗

Thinking About a Report

A report is a good way to share information about a subject. The title of a report gives the subject. The report is made up of paragraphs. The paragraphs give facts about the subject. The writer of a report tells where he or she got the information. The writer lists the titles and authors at the end of the report. Here is an example of a report.

Types of Clouds

There are three families of clouds. They are high, middle, and low. The high clouds are called cirrus clouds. They are made of ice crystals. They look something like thin, wispy hair. They form at least three miles above the earth.

The middle clouds have the prefix *alto-*, meaning high, to set them off from the lower clouds. One kind of middle cloud is the altostratus cloud. It forms a smooth, white sheet over the sky. The middle clouds form from one to four miles above the earth.

The low clouds have their bases anywhere from the surface of the earth to 6500 feet above the earth. Stratus is the name of one kind of low cloud. Stratus clouds stay near the surface of the earth. When people walk through fog, they are walking through a stratus cloud.

I got my information from these sources:
The Cloud Book by Julian May
Watch for the Clouds by Joan Lee
The World Book Encyclopedia, "Cloud"

Studying a Report Read the report above. Then answer these questions.

1. What is the subject of the report? **types of clouds**

2. What is the title? **"Types of Clouds"**

3. How many paragraphs does the report have? **three**

4. What is the first paragraph about? **cirrus clouds or high clouds**

5. What is the second paragraph about? **middle clouds**

6. What is the third paragraph about? **low clouds**

7. Where did the writer's information come from? **The Cloud Book by Julian May**
Watch for the Clouds by Joan Lee
The World Book Encyclopedia, "Cloud"

Prewriting: Choosing a Subject

Writing a Report
127

Sometimes you will need to find a subject for a report. Follow these three steps.

1. Make a list. List several subjects that interest you. Some might be from a chapter you are studying. List subjects you would like to know more about.

2. Use the library. Find out if there is enough information about your subjects. Use the card catalog to find books on your subjects. Look through them briefly. Read about your subjects in encyclopedias.

You may not find enough information about a subject. Cross it off your list.

If you find too much information, limit the subject. That is, find a smaller subject within it. A subject like "Insects" might be too big for a short report. You can limit the subject to "Life of a Mosquito."

3. Decide on a subject. Choose the one subject on your list that is most interesting to you.

Limiting a Subject for a Short Report Below are five sets of subjects. Underline the smallest or most limited subject in each set.

EXAMPLE: Flowers   <u>Parts of a Flower</u>   Flowers of America

1. Birds   <u>Penguins</u>   Cold Weather Birds

2. <u>The White House</u>   Washington, D.C.   Our Nation's Capital

3. Flying Insects   Bees   <u>How Bees Make Honey</u>

4. Sports   <u>How Basketball Began</u>   Basketball

5. <u>What Causes Cavities</u>   Teeth   Dentistry

Choosing an Interesting Subject List three subjects that you find interesting. You may find them in your social studies or science books. You may choose one of the subjects from the exercise above. You might choose a subject you know something about. Look for information in the library. If any subject is too big for a short report, limit it to one you can cover well. Choose one of the subjects for a report and circle it.   **Subjects will vary.**

1. _____

2. _____

3. _____

Prewriting: Finding Information

Writing a Report
128

Before you can write a report, you must read and collect information about your subject. Take notes to remember the information.

To take notes about information you find in a book, write the name of the book and the author at the top of a note card. If the book is an encyclopedia, write both the name of the encyclopedia and the name of the article. Then write a fact about the subject. Write the fact in your own words. Use a separate card for each fact.

You can also get information from people who are experts on your subject. If you talk to a person, take notes as you would from a book. Write the person's name and the date at the top of the card.

Taking Notes Read this paragraph from *The World Book Encyclopedia.* In the spaces below, write the name of the encyclopedia and the article. Then write one fact from the paragraph on each card in your own words.

> **LAVA** is molten rock that pours out of volcanoes or from cracks in the earth. It comes from deep in the earth where the heat is great. When lava first comes to the surface, it is red hot, reaching temperatures from seven to ten times hotter than boiling water.

Facts will vary.

The World Book Encyclopedia,
"Lava"

The World Book Encyclopedia,
"Lava"

Taking Notes for Your Report Find books with information about the topic you have chosen for a report. Use at least one book and one encyclopedia. Take at least six notes on separate note cards.

Skills Practice Book, Aqua Level
Copyright © by McDougal, Littell & Company

Prewriting: Sorting Notes

Writing a Report
129

Before you write your report, you must put your facts in order. Begin rereading your notes. Think about your main idea. Write at least three questions about the main idea of your report.

One writer chose to write about Venus's flytraps. She wrote these questions:

What is a Venus's flytrap?
What do its leaves look like?
How does it catch insects?

After you write your questions, sort your note cards. Put all the note cards that help to answer the first question in the first pile. Make a separate pile to answer each of the other questions. Some cards will probably not answer any of the questions. Put them in the last pile.

Sorting Notes Below are three questions that one writer wants to answer in a report. The questions are numbered 1, 2, and 3. Read each of the notes. Write a numeral on the line according to which question the note answers.

1. What were the homes of the California Indians like?
2. What were the homes of the Plains Indians like?
3. What were the homes of the Southwest Indians like?

____1____ The homes of the California Indians were covered with earth or brush.

____3____ The Indians of the Southwest lived in large houses.

____3____ The Southwest Indians made homes of stone and adobe.

____2____ The Plains Indians lived in tepees.

____1____ Some California Indians lived in simple shelters.

____2____ The tepees of the Plains Indians looked like tents.

____1____ Some California tribes had redwood plank houses.

____3____ Many Southwest Indians lived together in one house.

____2____ Buffalo skins covered the homes of the Plains Indians.

Sorting Your Notes Reread your note cards. Write at least three questions about the main idea of your report. Sort your cards into separate piles to answer each question.

Prewriting: Making an Outline

Writing a Report
130

Making an outline will help you write your report. When you write an outline, follow these steps.

1. Answer your questions. The writer of the report on Venus's flytraps wrote these answers:

> Venus's flytrap is a surprising plant.
> Leaves of the flytrap act like traps.
> Insect that lands on leaf becomes caught.

2. Write the outline. Use the answers to your questions as the main topics of your outline. Write the main idea from your first pile. Label it with a Roman numeral. Then write the facts from that pile as subtopics under the main topic. Label them until you have written all your main ideas and the subtopics under them.

3. Write the title telling the main idea of the report.

Below is the outline of the report on Venus's flytraps. Follow this form carefully when you write your own outline.

Title   Venus's Flytraps

Topic   I. Venus's flytrap is a surprising plant
   Subtopics   A. Venus's flytrap catches and eats insects
   B. Name of plant fits plant

Topic   II. Leaves of flytrap act like traps
   Subtopics   A. Leaves from three to six inches long
   B. Stickers at edges of leaves
   C. Six hairs growing on every leaf
   D. Leaves give off purple-colored juice

Topic   III. Insect that lands on leaf becomes caught
   Subtopics   A. Insect touching hairs triggers trap
   B. Rows of stickers cross and keep insect from flying away
   C. Insect becomes food for plant

Outlining Your Report Answer each of your questions. Make your outline. Use the answers as main topics. Use the facts from each group of cards as subtopics. Make sure your finished outline follows the outline form shown above. Write your outline on a separate sheet of paper.

Writing a Draft

Writing a Report

When you write your report, follow your outline. Write the first main topic as the topic sentence of your first paragraph. Remember to indent the first line of the paragraph. Then write other sentences to cover the subtopics under your main idea.

Next, indent and write the topic sentence for your second main idea. This will begin your second paragraph. Write the subtopics under the second main idea as sentences in your second paragraph.

Cover each main topic and the subtopics under it in a separate paragraph. You will have one paragraph for each main idea in your outline.

The third part of the outline on Venus's flytraps is given below, along with the draft of the paragraph written from it. Notice how the writer wrote complete sentences from each idea in the outline. This part of the draft will be revised later.

III. Insect that lands on leaf becomes caught

    A. Insect touching hairs triggers trap
    B. Rows of stickers cross and keep insect from flying away
    C. Insect becomes food for plant

    Any insect that lands on a leaf becomes caught. The insect touches one of the hairs and triggers the trap to shut. The rows of stickers cross each other. They keep the insect from flying away. The insect then becomes food for the plant.

Writing Your Draft Begin writing a draft of your report. Write the first paragraph on the lines below. Follow your outline closely. Use the main topics from your outline as the topic sentences in your report. Write a complete paragraph for every main topic in your outline. Finish your draft on your own paper.

_____
_____
_____
_____
_____
_____
_____

Revising a Report

Writing a Report 132

After you write your report, you should revise it. Ask yourself the following questions as you reread your report. Mark the changes in the report as you read it.

> **Guides for Revising**
>
> 1. Do all the paragraphs tell about the main idea of the report?
> 2. Does each paragraph include a topic sentence?
> 3. Do all the sentences in a paragraph stick to the main idea of the paragraph? Should any words or sentences be taken out?
> 4. Should any words or sentences be added to make the report clearer?
> 5. Is every group of words a complete sentence?
> 6. Does the title tell the main idea of your report?
> 7. Did you copy the facts correctly from your notes?

Here is one paragraph from the report on Venus's flytraps that has been revised. Notice that the writer added, took out, and changed words and sentences to make the paragraph clearer.

The leaves of the ^Venus's flytrap act like traps. The leaves ~~of the flytrap~~ are from three to six inches long. A row of stickers ~~is along the~~ ^lines both edges of ~~the leaves.~~ ^each leaf. Six ^slender hairs grow on every leaf. The leaves give off a purple-colored juice.^ that insects like to eat.

Revising a Report Rewrite the paragraph above with the revisions that are marked. Write the paragraph on the lines below. Notice how the changes improved the paragraph.

    The leaves of the Venus's flytrap act like traps. The leaves are from three to six inches long. A row of stickers lines both edges of each leaf. Six slender hairs grow on every leaf. The leaves give off a purple-colored juice that insects like to eat.

Revising Your Report Revise your report following the guides above. Use a different colored pencil or pen to make your changes.

Proofreading and Finishing a Report

After revising your report for ideas, you must proofread it. When you proofread your report, you are looking for mistakes. Ask yourself these questions as you proofread.

1. Is the first line of each paragraph indented?
2. Is every pronoun and verb used correctly?
3. Does every proper noun and sentence begin with a capital letter?
4. Are the words in the title capitalized correctly?
5. Are commas, apostrophes, and end marks used correctly?
6. Is every word spelled correctly?

At the end of your report, you must tell where you found your information. Give the titles and authors of any books you used. Give the names of encyclopedias and titles of the articles. Be sure to underline book titles, put quotation marks around names of articles, and capitalize them all correctly.

List your sources like this:

> I got my information from these sources:
> <u>The World of Plants</u> by Carol McGraw
> <u>The World Book Encyclopedia</u>, "Venus's Flytrap"

Read the finished report about Venus's flytraps below.

Venus's Flytraps

    The Venus's flytrap is a surprising plant. It is a plant that catches and eats insects. So you see, the name of this plant is a good one.
    The leaves of the Venus's flytrap act like traps. The leaves are from three to six inches long. A row of stickers lines both edges of each leaf. Six slender hairs grow on every leaf. The leaves give off a purple-colored juice that insects like to eat.
    When an insect lands on a leaf, it becomes caught. The insect touches one of the hairs. This triggers the trap shut. The rows of stickers cross each other like the fingers of two clasped hands. The crossed stickers keep the insect from flying out. The insect then becomes food for the plant. The Venus's flytrap lives on flies and other insects it catches in this way.

> I got my information from these sources:
> <u>The World of Plants</u> by Carol McGraw
> <u>The World Book Encyclopedia</u>, "Venus's Flytrap"

Proofreading Your Report If your own report is too marked-up with revisions to read easily, copy it on another paper. Then proofread it, following the questions on this page.
    Make a clean final copy of your report. At the end of the report, list your sources.

Review: Writing a Report

Thinking About Reports Read this paragraph from a report about Conestoga wagons. Conestoga wagons were the type of wagon that many settlers used to travel west in the 1800's. Then answer the question below.

> The most unusual feature of the wagon was the cloth cover. The cover was made of canvas, a heavy cloth. The cover had to be sturdy to keep out rain and dust. The cloth was held up by hickory strips bent into arches called bows. The cover was anchored to the bottom of the wagon so it would not fly off. The cover protected the passengers and their supplies.

What is the main idea of the paragraph? **the cover of a Conestoga wagon**

Making an Outline Below is the unfinished outline for the paragraph above. Each topic should tell one fact from the paragraph. Finish the outline.

II. The wagon cover

    A. **made of canvas, a heavy cloth**

    B. **sturdy to keep out rain and dust**

    C. **held up by hickory bows**

    D. **anchored to bottom of wagon**

    E. **protected passengers and supplies**

Revising Rewrite the following sentences from the report. Correct errors in grammar, capitalization, punctuation, and spelling.

1. Oxen pulled the wagons they were yoked togeter.

   Oxen pulled the wagons. They were yoked together.

2. Oxen were more slower than horses but they were sturdyer animals.

   Oxen were slower than horses, but they were sturdier animals.

3. The wagons carried everything that familys needed for there new life.

   The wagons carried everything that families needed for their new life.

4. Conestoga wagons were very uncomfterble to Travel in.

   Conestoga wagons were very uncomfortable to travel in.

5. Sometimes the axles or weels breaked.

   Sometimes the axles or wheels broke.

The Speaker in Poems

Enjoying Poetry

The person who does the talking in a poem is called the **speaker**. In some poems, the speaker tells a story. In other poems, he or she talks to someone else in the poem. Sometimes the speaker just states his or her feelings.

When you read a poem, first decide who the speaker is. Is the speaker a child, an adult, or an animal? Could the speaker be a father or a teacher or a cook? Then think about whom the speaker is talking to, if anyone. Finally, think about what the speaker's feelings are.

Learning About the Speaker Read the following poem. Then answer the questions below.

I Never Win at Parties

I never win at parties.
I never win at all.
Someone gets the prizes.
Someone wins the ball.
Someone gets the roses
Off the birthday cake.
I don't get the roses;
I get the stomachache.
Someone pins the tail
On the donkey's seat.
When I pin the donkey,
It ends up on his feet.
Someone drops the clothespins
Right where they should go.
I can't hit the bottle,
Even bending low.
I do not know the reason
Unless it's that I'm small,
Why I don't win at parties.
I just don't win at all.
—MARCI RIDLON

1. Who is the speaker in the poem? **a child**

2. What games does the speaker lose? **Pin the Tail on the Donkey, Clothespin-Bottle Game**

3. Is the speaker telling a story, expressing happiness, or complaining? **complaining**

4. How do you think the speaker feels? **Answers will vary, but should include disappointment, frustration, or sadness.**

5. Have you ever felt the same way? When? **Answers will vary.**

Pictures in Poetry

A poem often gives a picture in words. The picture may be still, or it may be moving. Notice how the following poem describes one single, still picture.

> A spark in the sun,
> This tiny flower has roots
> Deep in the cool earth.
> —HARRY BEHN

The poet compares the flower to a spark in the sun rooted in the cool earth. It is a still picture. Could you draw this picture?

The pictures in some poems do not stay still. The poem presents a moving picture rather than a still picture. Read this poem and feel the motion.

> **Sleet Storm**
>
> TIC-TIC-TIC!
> The sound of the sleet
> Fell like the beat
> Of tiny feet,
> Racing and chasing down the street.
> —JAMES S. TIPPETT

Understanding Pictures in Poetry Read the following poem. Try to form a picture in your mind. Then answer the questions below.

> **Shadows**
>
> Chunks of night
> Melt
> In the morning sun.
> One lonely one
> Grows legs
> And follows me
> To school.
> —PATRICIA HUBBELL

1. What is the title of this poem? **Shadows**

2. What does the poet mean by "chunks of night"? **pieces of darkness**

3. What happens to the "chunks of night"? **They "melt" into daylight.**

4. What does the last chunk become? **the speaker's shadow**

5. Is the picture in this poem a still or a moving picture? **moving**

Sound Patterns in Poetry

Poets use sound in special ways. One sound pattern that poets use often is **rhyme.** Words with the same ending sound rhyme, such as *spell* and *tell*. Poets often use rhyming words at the ends of lines. Notice the rhymes in this poem.

Extremes

A little boy once played so loud
That the thunder, up in a thundercloud,
Said, "Since *I* can't be heard, why, then
I'll never, never thunder again!"
—JAMES WHITCOMB RILEY

The rhyming words are *loud* and *thundercloud,* and *then* and *again.* The rhymes form a pattern. The last words in the first and second lines rhyme. The last words in the third and fourth lines rhyme.

Alliteration is another sound pattern. **Alliteration** is the repeating of the same consonant sound at the beginnings of words. Here is an example: "Sing a song of sixpence." Alliteration can add to the meaning of the poem.

Listening for Sound Patterns Read the following poem aloud. Then answer the questions below it.

Summer

When summer blues the skies
And thrushes sing for hours,
And gold and orange butterflies
Float by like flying flowers . . .
Although I squint my eyes
The way a thinker does,
Somehow, I just can't realize
That winter ever was.
—KAYE STARBIRD

1. List three sets of rhyming words from this poem. One set has four words.

   skies   **hours**   **does**

   butterflies   **flowers**   **was**

   eyes

   realize

2. In the fourth line, what consonant sound is repeated for alliteration? **fl**

3. What are the speaker's feelings about summer? **Answers will vary. Speaker feels summer might go on forever.**

Rhythm in Poetry

Just like music, poems have rhythm. **Rhythm** is the pattern of strong and weak beats in a poem. The rhythm is very strong in some poems. When you read that kind of poem out loud, you can hear the beats.

Each group of lines in a poem is called a **stanza.** The strong beats of the first stanza of the following poem were marked for you. Read the poem aloud. Tap out the strong beats as you read.

Windy Nights

Whenéver the móon and stárs are sét,
    Whenéver the wínd is hígh,
Áll night lóng in the dárk and wét,
    A mán goes ríding bý.
Láte in the níght when the fíres are oút,
Whý does he gállop and gállop abóut?

Whenever the trees are crying aloud,
    And ships are tossed at sea,
By, on the highway, low and loud,
    By at the gallop goes he.
By at the gallop he goes, and then
By he comes back at the gallop again.
    —ROBERT LOUIS STEVENSON

Can you hear the beats of the poem? Do they remind you of a galloping horse?

Marking the Rhythm As you read this nursery rhyme, tap the beats very softly. Mark the strong beats in each line.

Máry hád a líttle lámb,

Its fléece was whíte as snów,

And éverywhére that Máry wént,

The lámb was súre to gó.

Review: Enjoying Poetry

Understanding Poetry Read the following poems and answer the questions below them.

Back and Forth

Báck and fórth
go the férries,
báck and fórth
from shóre to shóre,
hauling people, trucks and autos,
back and forth
from shore to shore.
　　—LUCY SPRAGUE MITCHELL

1. Does this poem present a still or moving picture? __**moving**__

2. Put an accent mark above the strong beats in the first four lines of the poem above.

The Willows

By the little river,
　Still and deep and brown,
Grow the graceful willows,
　Gently dipping down.
　　—WALTER PRICHARD EATON

3. Does this poem present a still or moving picture? __**still**__

4. Which words rhyme? __**brown, down**__

5. What consonant sound is repeated in the third line? __**gr**__

6. Which consonant sound is repeated in the last line? __**d**__

If You Pinch a Dinosaur

If you pinch a Dinosaur
You might get him kinda sore:
He might bite and he might roar!
Better pinch the kid next door.
　　—SHEL SILVERSTEIN

7. Whom is the speaker addressing? __**the reader**__

8. Is the speaker scared, serious, joking, or sad? __**joking**__

Capitalizing Names of People and Pets

Using Capital Letters
140

The use of capital letters is called **capitalization.** The following rules tell you when to capitalize words.

A **proper noun** is the name of a particular person, place, or thing. **Begin every proper noun with a capital letter.**

  William Penn Arkansas Cadillac

Capitalize the names of people and pets. Begin every word and initial of a person's name with a capital letter. Put a period after each initial.

  Helen Keller George C. Marshall Snoopy

Words like *Miss, Doctor,* and *Senator* are called **titles.** Some titles have short forms, called **abbreviations.**

Capitalize titles and their abbreviations when you use them with names. Put a period after every abbreviation.

  Prime Minister Margaret Thatcher Dr. McLaughlin

Always capitalize the word *I*.

Using Capital Letters in Names

Find the words in the following sentences that should be capitalized. Write the words on the blanks. Use capital letters where they are needed.

1. ramon and i named our cat mustard.

   Ramon and I named our cat Mustard.

2. a. a. milne wrote about a teddy bear called winnie the pooh.

   A. A. Milne wrote about a teddy bear called Winnie the Pooh.

3. dr. seuss has written many books for children.

   Dr. Seuss has written many books for children.

4. mother teresa has helped poor people all over the world.

   Mother Teresa has helped poor people all over the world.

5. mrs. anderson baked a cake for her daughter kathy.

   Mrs. Anderson baked a cake for her daughter Kathy.

Capitalizing Names of Places and Things

Using Capital Letters
141

1. **Capitalize names of days, holidays, and months.** Capitalize their abbreviations also. Do not capitalize the names of seasons, such as spring.

    Monday   Thurs.   Labor Day   September   Dec.

2. **Capitalize the names of buildings and streets.**

    Lincoln Memorial   Park Ave.

3. **Capitalize names of cities, states, and countries.** Also capitalize both letters of the two-letter postal abbreviations for states.

    Helena, Montana   Maine = ME
    London, England   Oklahoma = OK

4. **Capitalize names for people of particular countries.**

    Japanese   Americans   English

The names of particular places and things may have more than one word. Capitalize all important words. Do not capitalize *the, of,* or *in.*

Using Capital Letters for Particular Places and Things Find the words in the following sentences that should be capitalized. Write the words on the blanks. Use capital letters where they are needed.

1. The halloween party will be on friday, october 31.

    Halloween, Friday, October

2. I will meet you at the corner of main street and chestnut avenue.

    Main Street, Chestnut Avenue

3. Dennis was born in anchorage, alaska.

    Anchorage, Alaska

4. Paper was invented by the chinese in ancient times.

    Chinese

5. In august, Janet climbed the eiffel tower in paris, france.

    August, Eiffel Tower, Paris, France

Capitalizing First Words (1)

Using Capital Letters
142

Here are three rules for using capital letters in certain places.
Begin every sentence with a capital letter.

> Today is my birthday.   When is your birthday?

Capitalize the beginning of every direct quotation. When you write the exact words that somebody said, you are **quoting** that person. The words are a **direct quotation.** Notice how the capital letters and quotation marks (" ") set off the direct quotation.

> Don asked, "What time is it?"
> "What time is it?" asked Don.

Capitalize the first word in most lines of poetry.

> Red sky at night
> Is the sailor's delight;
> Red sky at morning,
> Sailor, take warning!

Using Capital Letters in Sentences and Quotations Underline every word that should be capitalized.

1. <u>did</u> anybody bring a can opener?
2. <u>michael</u> said, "<u>this</u> hill is perfect for sledding."
3. "<u>who</u> was knocking at the door?" <u>lola</u> asked.
4. "<u>may</u> I borrow your sister's tennis racket?" <u>sheila</u> asked.
5. "<u>my</u> tire is flat again," <u>benjamin</u> complained.

Using Capital Letters in Poetry Copy the following poem. Use capital letters correctly.

> who has seen the wind?
> neither I nor you:
> but when the leaves hang trembling,
> the wind is passing through.
>   —CHRISTINA ROSSETTI

Who has seen the wind?

Neither I nor you:

But when the leaves hang trembling,

The wind is passing through.

Capitalizing First Words (2)

Using Capital Letters
143

Here are two more rules for using capital letters in certain positions.

Capitalize the first word in the greeting of a letter.

    Dear Regina,   Dear Sir:

Capitalize the first word in the closing of a letter.

    Your friend,   Sincerely yours,

Using Capital Letters in Sentences and Letters Copy the following letter in correct letter form. Use capital letters where they are needed.

                                                january 13, 1987

dear brian,

    last week norman and i got to school early. the whole playground was icy. we ran and slid on the ice. at first, it was fun. then norman fell, and his head hit the pavement. he didn't cut himself, but he kept saying, "my head hurts." he had to go to the hospital for two days. now he feels better.

                                                your friend,
                                                Carlos

                                                January 13, 1987

Dear Brian,

    Last week Norman and I got to school early. The whole playground was icy. We ran and slid on the ice. At first, it was fun. Then Norman fell, and his head hit the pavement. He didn't cut himself, but he kept saying, "My head hurts." He had to go to the hospital for two days. Now he feels better.

                                                Your friend,

                                                Carlos

Capitalizing Titles

Using Capital Letters
144

Capitalize the first word, the last word, and any other important words in a title. Do not capitalize a little word such as *in, of, for, a, the,* or *by,* unless it comes first or last.

    Treasure Island   (movie)
    Wide World of Sports   (television program)

Put quotation marks around the titles of short works, like stories, poems, and reports. Underline the titles of television programs and of long works, such as books, movies, and magazines. When they are printed in books, these titles are set in italics instead of being underlined.

Using Capital Letters in Titles
Copy the following titles. Capitalize them correctly. Copy the quotation marks and underlining.

1. "little red riding hood"   (story)

   "Little Red Riding Hood"

2. never cry wolf   (movie)

   <u>Never Cry Wolf</u>

3. jack and jill   (magazine)

   <u>Jack and Jill</u>

4. "the blind men and the elephant"   (poem)

   "The Blind Men and the Elephant"

5. the today show   (television program)

   <u>The Today Show</u>

6. the voyages of dr. dolittle   (book)

   <u>The Voyages of Dr. Dolittle</u>

7. "our first thanksgiving"   (report)

   "Our First Thanksgiving"

8. "the princess and the pea"   (story)

   "The Princess and the Pea"

9. the seventh voyage of sinbad   (movie)

   <u>The Seventh Voyage of Sinbad</u>

10. the middle moffat   (book)

    <u>The Middle Moffat</u>

Mixed Practice: Using Capital Letters

Using Capital Letters Copy each item, capitalizing words as necessary.

1. dr. jennings went to the university of new mexico.
   (D, J, U, N, M)

2. edgar allan poe wrote a scary story called "the pit and the pendulum."
   (E, A, P, T, P, P)

3. the poem "trees" by joyce kilmer begins with these lines.
   "I think that i shall never see
   a poem lovely as a tree."
   (T, T, J, K, I, A)

4. carla anne embroidered a sampler with her initials, c.a.t.
   (C, A, CAT)

5. again, julian said, "you can say that again."
   (A, J, Y)

6. will your trip to st. louis in april take you through texas?
   (W, S, L, A, T)

7. i wrote a song called "what a beautiful day."
   (I, W, B, D)

8. the spanish-speaking family on sixth street visited puerto rico.
   (T, S, S, P, R)

9. my letter from rob began with "dear ms. miss."
   (M, R, D, M, M)

10. mother and dad are going to lecture at the art institute of chicago.
    (M, D, A, I, C)

Using Capital Letters in Writing

Choose one of the three activities below. Do your writing on a separate sheet of paper. Remember to use capital letters correctly in sentences, proper nouns, and titles. **Answers will vary.**

1. Think about a trip you have taken lately. Where did you go? Whom did you go with? What cities or buildings did you visit? What did you see? Did you visit someone?

   Write at least five sentences about your trip. Answer as many of the questions above as possible. If you like, draw a map that shows where you've been.

2. Think about a book you have read and enjoyed lately. Write the name of the book here.

   _____

   On another paper, write about the book. Answer these six questions. Use complete sentences.

   What is the title of your book?
   Who were some of the characters in it?
   Where did your book take place?
   What were some of the things that happened in it?
   What did some of the characters say?
   Why did you like this book?

3. Imagine that you are a character on your favorite television show. Write a conversation you would have with another character on the same show.

Review: Using Capital Letters

Using Capital Letters Correctly In each sentence or phrase below, underline all words that should be capitalized.

1. <u>harriet</u> <u>tubman</u> was a brave woman.
2. <u>melissa</u> took her dog, <u>cocoa</u>, to the vet, <u>dr.</u> <u>tristan</u>.
3. <u>many</u> <u>dutch</u> from <u>amsterdam</u>, <u>holland</u>, settled in <u>new</u> <u>york</u>.
4. <u>in</u> one <u>greek</u> myth, <u>hercules</u> had to kill a nine-headed monster.
5. <u>president</u> <u>reagan</u> has a dog named <u>liberty</u>.
6. <u>my</u> appointment with <u>mayor</u> <u>hayes</u> is <u>wednesday</u>, <u>january</u> 9.
7. <u>in</u> one movie, <u>superman</u> flew to the <u>world</u> <u>trade</u> <u>center</u>.
8. <u>marchette</u> <u>chute</u> is an <u>american</u> writer.
9. <u>the</u> <u>russians</u> sent the first man into space.
10. <u>there</u> was an old man from <u>peru</u>
    <u>who</u> dreamed he was eating his shoe;
    <u>he</u> woke in a fright
    <u>in</u> the middle of the night
    <u>and</u> found it was perfectly true.
    —ANONYMOUS
11. <u>dear</u> <u>nora</u>,
12. <u>yours</u> truly,
13. <u>dear</u> sir or <u>madam</u>:
14. <u>sincerely</u>,
15. *<u>tuck</u> <u>everlasting</u>*   (book)
16. "<u>foods</u> of <u>many</u> <u>countries</u>"   (report)
17. *<u>growing</u> <u>pains</u>*   (television program)
18. "<u>stopping</u> by <u>woods</u> on a <u>snowy</u> <u>evening</u>"   (poem)
19. *<u>child</u> <u>life</u>*   (magazine)
20. *<u>escape</u> to <u>witch</u> <u>mountain</u>*   (movie)

The Period

1. Use a period (.) at the end of statements and most commands and requests. If you are reading aloud, the period tells you to drop your voice.

2. Use a period after an initial in a name, such as E. B. White.

3. Use a period after many abbreviations. Here are some examples.

TITLES		GEOGRAPHICAL TERMS		MEASURES	
Mister	Mr.	Street	St.	inch(es)	in.
Mistress	Mrs.	Avenue	Ave.	mile(s)	mi.
(no long form)	Ms.	Texas	Tex.	cup(s)	c.
Doctor	Dr.	Illinois	Ill.	ounce(s)	oz.
Reverend	Rev.	North	N. or No.	pounds(s)	lb.

Some abbreviations do not use periods.

Zone Improvement Plan	ZIP	Texas	TX
miles per hour	mph	Illinois	IL

4. Use a period after each numeral or letter that shows a division in an outline. Follow this form when you write an outline.

Leaders of the American Revolution
  I. In the North
    A. Benjamin Franklin
    B. Samuel Adams
  II. In the South
    A. Thomas Jefferson
    B. George Washington

Using Periods Correctly Supply periods where they are needed in the following outline, phrases, and sentences.

1. Sea Animals
  I. Large fish
    A. Sharks
    B. Swordfish
  II. Mammals
    A. Dolphins
    B. Whales

2. 5 lb, 11 oz.

3. 2 doz. doughnuts

4. Wed., Apr. 16

5. P.O. Box 80

6. 3 ft., 7 in.

7. N. Oak Ave.

8. I will see Dr. Page tomorrow at 3:00 P.M.

9. Gunpowder was invented in China about 850 A.D.

10. The package for Rev. Grant arrived C.O.D.

The Question Mark

Building Punctuation Power

● **Use a question mark (?) at the end of every question.** If you are reading aloud, the question mark tells you to raise your voice.

   Where is my pen?

Using Question Marks Correctly Supply either a period or a question mark at the end of each sentence.

1. Have you ever had pumpkin bread?
2. How do they measure the speed of a pitcher's throw?
3. That monster movie scared me.
4. How long have dinosaurs been extinct?
5. What is the address of the White House?
6. David shined his old shoes.
7. Samantha is the catcher on our softball team.
8. Does the sun ever shine during a rain shower?
9. When do we go on daylight savings time?
10. Do you hear the harmony in this song?
11. Fog is really a low-lying cloud.
12. Is Bruce coming to the skating rink?
13. German shepherds are used as guide dogs.
14. Why were you late?
15. A greenhouse is warm and damp inside.
16. Who painted the ceiling of the Sistine Chapel?
17. Can you use this type of computer?
18. My brother delivers papers early every morning.
19. How far away is the moon?
20. The blueberries were delicious.

The Exclamation Point

Use an exclamation point (!) at the end of an exclamation or a command that shows strong feeling. If you are reading aloud, the exclamation point tells you to show surprise, fear, or other strong feeling in your voice.

What an exciting game that was!
Be careful climbing that ladder!

Using Exclamation Points Correctly Supply either a period, question mark, or exclamation point at the end of each sentence.

1. How hot this soup is!
2. What ingredients do you like on a pizza?
3. Move out of the way quickly!
4. Holly turned a somersault.
5. Have you seen a rainbow lately?
6. Ms. Beyer typed a business letter.
7. Can Sam play the piano?
8. Stop running in the hallway!
9. Grandmother's vase is falling!
10. The squirrel buried an acorn.
11. How noisy this crowd is!
12. The oil has caught on fire!
13. Frank collected seashells on the beach.
14. Did you enjoy the magic show?
15. Lightning just struck that tree!
16. How tiny the dollhouse lamp is!
17. Do you read many books in the summer?
18. Ellen is a good soccer player.
19. Have you ever made a soap carving?
20. What a nice gift you brought!

The Comma (1)

Building Punctuation Power
151

The comma (,) signals a pause in a sentence. If you are reading aloud, the comma tells you to pause briefly.

1. Use a comma in dates to separate the day of the month from the year. If the date is written in the middle of the sentence, place a comma after the year also.

John F. Kennedy became President on January 20, 1961.
On October 31, 1864, Nevada became a state.

2. Use a comma to separate the name of a city from the state or country in which it is located. If the name is written in the middle of a sentence, place a comma after the state or country.

The first Thanksgiving took place in Plymouth, Massachusetts.
Rome, Italy, has a very colorful history.

Using Commas Correctly Supply commas in the following sentences where needed.

1. Mitzu moved into her new house on June 2, 1986.

2. Shel took a bus to Davenport, Iowa, to visit his grandmother.

3. On April 14, 1865, President Lincoln was shot.

4. London, England, is one of the biggest cities in the world.

5. That movie was filmed in Cairo, Egypt.

6. The twins were born in Portland, Maine, on August 14, 1982.

7. My family went camping near Jackson Hole, Wyoming.

8. The Leaning Tower is in Pisa, Italy.

9. My grandparents arrived in America on September 8, 1946.

10. Many people ski in Vail, Colorado.

11. Milan, Ohio, is the birthplace of Thomas Edison.

12. A terrible earthquake struck San Francisco on April 18, 1906.

13. Disneyland is located in Anaheim, California.

14. Our national anthem was written on September 14, 1814.

15. St. Augustine, Florida, was founded on August 28, 1565.

The Comma (2)

Building Punctuation Power

1. Use a comma to set off the name of a person spoken to.

You are a good helper, Eric.
Tracey, will you wait for me?

2. Use a comma after *yes, no,* or *well* at the beginning of a sentence.

Yes, I can come to your party.
No, the movie has not started yet.
Well, we tried.

3. Use a comma to set apart words in a series. Place the comma after all but the last word in the series. A series lists three or more items.

Tara brought hamburgers, buns, and carrot sticks to the picnic.

4. Use a comma after the first complete thought in a sentence with two thoughts. These sentences are **compound** sentences. The comma is placed before the word *and, but,* or *or.*

The boys went to the fair, and they had a good time.
The sun was shining, but it was still cold.
We can ride our bikes, or we can walk.

Using Commas Correctly Supply commas in the following sentences where they are needed.

1. Well, our team will win the pennant next year.

2. The oxen smelled water, and they moved faster.

3. Amy, have you practiced for the race?

4. Yes, the home run ball broke the window.

5. Write down the answer, or you might forget it.

6. Larry, Curly, and Moe were the Three Stooges.

7. You sing very well, Justin.

8. No, I have never ridden a horse.

9. Jesse and Liz washed the fruit, and we each had a piece.

10. Many Jamaicans pick mangos, bananas, and cashews from their own trees.

The Comma (3)

1. Use a comma after the greeting of a friendly letter, and after the closing of every letter.

Dear Bonnie,   Yours truly,

2. Use a comma to set off a direct quotation from the rest of the sentence. The comma is placed before the quotation marks.

"I enjoy gymnastics," Pam announced.
Ginny answered, "The stunts are very difficult."

Using Commas Correctly Supply commas where they are needed in the following sentences and letter.

1. "This coat is old-fashioned," complained Angela.

2. Ruth said, "Let's rake the leaves."

3. "I overslept," explained Martin.

4. "Please open the window," said Mrs. Porter.

5. Neil said, "Let me help you."

6. Luis called, "Strike him out!"

7. "The bill is six dollars," the cashier said.

8.   July 8, 1987

Dear Mom,

   Yes, I am having a good time here at camp. I thought I might be bored, but there are many activities for us. We take swimming lessons, riding lessons, and crafts. Today we went for a hike up Mount Jefferson. The mountain is steep, and I was afraid I wouldn't finish the climb. I finally reached the top and shouted, "I made it!" Well, I was proud of myself.

   I hope you, Dad, and Brent are fine.

               Your daughter,
               Devonne

The Apostrophe

Building Punctuation Power
154

The **apostrophe (')** is used for two different purposes. It is used to show possession, and it is used in contractions.

Using the Apostrophe To Show Possession A **possessive** is a word that shows ownership or possession.

To form the possessive of a singular noun, add an apostrophe and an *s*.

woman + **'s** = woman's   Russ + **'s** = Russ's

To form the possessive of a plural noun that does not end in *s*, add an apostrophe and an *s*.

women + **'s** = women's   children + **'s** = children's

To form the possessive of a plural noun that ends in *s*, add only an apostrophe.

boys + **'** = boys'   girls + **'** = girls'

Using Apostrophes To Show Possession Write the possessive forms of these nouns on the blanks.

1. baby — **baby's**
2. men — **men's**
3. students — **students'**
4. neighbors — **neighbors'**
5. James — **James's**
6. deer — **deer's**

Using the Apostrophe in Contractions A **contraction** is a word made by combining two words and leaving out a letter or letters. **Use an apostrophe in a contraction to show where a letter or letters have been left out.**

Here are some contractions that are used often:

haven't	have not	it's	it is, it has
can't	can not	we're	we are
won't	will not	you'd	you would
he'll	he will	I'm	I am

Using Apostrophes in Contractions Write each of the following phrases as a contraction.

1. is not — **isn't**
2. she has — **she's**
3. I would — **I'd**
4. you will — **you'll**
5. it is — **it's**
6. they are — **they're**

Quotation Marks

Use quotation marks (" ") before and after the words of every direct quotation. A **direct quotation** means the exact words a person says.

 Sharon said, "This is a good book."
 "I have not read it," replied Mike.

Follow these guides for writing quotations.

1. Place only the speaker's words inside the quotation marks.

2. Begin the quotation with a capital letter.

3. If the quotation comes at the end of the sentence, put a comma before the quotation. The end mark for the sentence usually is placed inside the quotation marks.

 Ira called, "Here comes the helicopter."

4. If the quotation comes at the beginning of the sentence, put the end mark for the quotation inside the quotation marks. Put the end mark for the rest of the sentence at the end of the sentence.

 "Can you swim fifty yards?" Bert asked.

 "Your lemon pie is delicious!" my mother exclaimed.

 "The baby has fallen asleep," Randi said.

Notice that the third example has a statement inside the quotation marks. In this situation, use a comma instead of a period to set off the statement from the rest of the sentence.

Using Quotation Marks Correctly Supply quotation marks where they are needed.

1. Rodney asked, "Do you collect stamps?"

2. "I can climb that tree," boasted Gail.

3. Peter said, "I have a new pair of roller skates."

4. "Please set the table," my father requested.

5. Martha cried, "Let's build a snowman!"

6. "I have a pet hamster named George," announced Jennifer.

7. "We are lost!" shouted Mark.

8. Felicia asked, "When does the bus arrive?"

9. "What is a peso?" Daniel asked.

10. "This television show is boring," Lucy complained.

Quotation Marks and Underlining in Titles

Building Punctuation Power 156

Quotation Marks in Titles Put quotation marks around the titles of poems, stories, and other short works.

"Wynken, Blynken, and Nod"   (poem)
"The Ugly Duckling"   (story)
"Sea Monsters"   (student report)

Using Quotation Marks in Titles Correctly
Supply quotation marks where they are needed.

1. Kim enjoyed writing her report called "Climbing Mt. Everest."

2. "The Lion's Whiskers" is an African folk story.

3. I laughed at the story called "The Emperor's New Clothes."

4. Our class read the poem called "Spring Song."

5. "The Legend of Sleepy Hollow" is a scary story.

6. Everyone enjoyed the poem called "The Lobster Quadrille."

7. Irene read an American story called "Paul Bunyan."

8. Tony wrote a report called "Alligators and Crocodiles."

Underlining in Titles Underline the titles of books and other long works. When these titles are set in print, they are in *italics*.

Ben and Me   (book title in writing)
Ben and Me   (book title in print)
National Geographic   (magazine)
Bambi   (movie)

Using Underlining Correctly
Use quotation marks or underlining as needed.

1. *T.V. Guide*   (magazine)
2. *The Borrowers*   (book)
3. "The Lamb"   (poem)
4. "African Wildlife"   (report)
5. *Mr. Popper's Penguins*   (book)
6. "The Talking Cat"   (story)
7. *The Parent Trap*   (movie)
8. "Zlateh the Goat"   (story)
9. *Rascal*   (book)
10. *Popular Mechanics*   (magazine)
11. "Weather Forecasting"   (report)
12. "Frog Went A-Courtin'"   (poem)

The Colon

Building Punctuation Power

There are several uses for the **colon (:)**. Here are two of them.

1. **Use a colon after the greeting in a business letter.**

   Dear Miss Ross: Dear Madam:

2. **Use a colon between numerals that tell the hour and the minutes.**
   Remember to use periods in the abbreviations *A.M.* and *P.M.*

   5:30 A.M.   10:15 P.M.

Using Colons Correctly Copy this business letter on the lines below. Use colons and periods where they are needed.

September 17, 1986

Dear Mrs. Fallon:

    This is to inform you of the new schedule at the Carnegie Public Library. The library will be open from 9:00 A.M. to 5:30 P.M. on Mondays, Wednesdays, and Fridays. It will be open from 9:00 A.M. to 8:00 P.M. on Tuesdays and Thursdays. The new hours on Saturday will be from 11:00 A.M. to 3:00 P.M. Please announce these new hours to your class.

Truly yours,

Ms. Marian Wilson

Mixed Practice (1): Building Punctuation Power

Using End Marks Add a period, question mark, or exclamation point at the end of each sentence.

1. Maple trees lose their leaves in winter.
2. How much snow fell last night?
3. How quickly my puppy grew!
4. Did anyone bring goggles to the beach?
5. Cardinals are easy to see against a background of snow.
6. Janet lost her guitar pick.
7. Barry bought some black swim fins.
8. Do we have enough wood for a fire tonight?
9. What a strong finish your team made!
10. Who will videotape our play?

Using End Marks and Commas Insert end marks and commas where they are needed in each sentence.

1. June 21 is the longest day in the year, and December 21 is the shortest.
2. Timothy, will you come home early this afternoon?
3. San Diego, California, is south of Long Beach.
4. No, I have not swept the sidewalk yet.
5. Have the tulips, daffodils, and forsythia bloomed?
6. Young kittens are fun, but older cats sleep most of the time.
7. Ellen, stop that racket this minute!
8. On January 20, 1986, I went to Washington, D.C.
9. Owen, please buy milk, orange juice, cheese, and eggs on your way home.
10. Well, my math is done, but I still have some reading.

Mixed Practice (2): Building Punctuation Power

Using Punctuation Insert end marks, commas, apostrophes, colons, question marks, or underlining as needed in the following sentences.

1. Dawn said, "We're going to move to Memphis, Tennessee."
2. Yes, give tickets to Robb, Cindy, Shelly, and Dan.
3. Ms. Hayes's report was dated February 12, 1986.
4. Ron ate breakfast, and then he brushed his teeth.
5. Well, Sandy likes pudding, but he loves ice cream.
6. Roses, daisies, and carnations are in the bouquet.
7. "Kathy, your train leaves at 2:35 P.M.," Dad said.
8. "Has anyone seen Jackie?" Mrs. Brown asked.
9. Corey was reading the story "How the Leopard Got His Spots" from <u>The Jungle Book</u>.
10. "Jimmy, don't run into the street!" screamed Carlie.

Using Punctuation in a Letter Read this letter. Insert punctuation marks where needed.

107 Winding Lane
Storybook, California 09736
August 13, 1986

Mr. Jack Sprat
329 Fit Street
Joggerville, Maryland 21703

Dear Mr. Sprat:

    We received your order for fat-free beef today. I am sorry to say that the beef we send you will not be totally free of fat. We will, however, give you as lean a cut as possible. Might we suggest that another member of your family eat the parts that are not lean enough for you?

    Thank you for your order. It shall be sent at 3:00 P.M. today and should arrive by 4:00 P.M. tomorrow.

Sincerely,

H.D. Dock
Mother Goose Meat Company

Using Punctuation in Writing

Building Punctuation Power
160

Choose one of the three activities below. Be sure to use punctuation marks correctly. Try to use each of these marks at least once: period, question mark, exclamation point, comma, apostrophe, quotation marks, and underlining. Use the space below. **Answers will vary.**

1. Write a comic strip. Draw characters, and write what they say in bubbles above their heads. Include all four kinds of sentences in their conversation.

2. Listen carefully to a conversation between two other people. They can be adults or children. Then test your memory by writing down everything they said. After you have written what you remember, go back and add the correct punctuation to your written conversation. You have become a human tape recorder!

3. Make up an advertisement for a product from a foreign country. It can be food or clothing or any other item. In your advertisement, quote a happy customer. Try to use as many kinds of punctuation in the ad as you can. Make it colorful and eyecatching.

Review: Building Punctuation Power

Punctuating Sentences Correctly Punctuate the following sentences correctly. Use all the punctuation marks you have studied.

1. My younger sister was born on December 27, 1982.
2. Dr. Webb helped me with my report, "How Our Muscles Work."
3. No, we haven't found Carla's cat yet.
4. Cliff will give this note to Ms. Wendell.
5. *Johnny Tremain* is a book about Boston, Massachusetts, in 1775.
6. What a large fish you caught!
7. Eva, please read the next question.
8. Yes, I will write a thank-you note.
9. We need glue, scissors, and crayons for our art project.
10. Bring your bat, ball, and mitt, and we will play baseball.
11. Mr. Buckley read to us the poem "The Pied Piper of Hamelin."
12. It is Mrs. Anderson's birthday, and the class bought a present.
13. The weather forecaster predicted a sunny day, but it rained.
14. "I adore you, Kermit!" exclaimed Miss Piggy.
15. No, I haven't seen the movie *Darby O'Gill and the Little People*.
16. "Children, please be quiet," said Mr. Owen.
17. No, I can't go skating today.
18. The mother bear said, "This porridge is too cold."
19. Timmy likes the story called "Seven in One Blow."
20. Gwen is reading an article in the magazine *Children's Digest*.
21. If it is 8:00 A.M. in New York, what time is it in Chicago?
22. Well, I think *The Black Stallion* starts at 8:00 P.M.
23. We can take the bus at 11:30 A.M. or we can wait until 12:45 P.M.
24. The alarm clock rang at 7:00 A.M., and Don got out of bed.
25. Mother said, "We will eat supper at 5:30 P.M."

The Parts of a Friendly Letter (1)

Writing a Letter
162

There are five main parts in a letter. Here is a sample letter.

[Sample handwritten letter showing:]

Heading: 10 Park Street
Clinton, Massachusetts 01510
September 10, 1987

Greeting: Dear Betsy,

Body: My family and I went to an amusement park last Sunday. We had a great time! The roller coaster was my favorite ride.
How are you? Write and tell me what you have done this summer.

Closing: Your friend,
Signature: Laura

The first part of a letter is the **heading.** The heading tells your address and the date. Write the heading in the top right-hand corner. Include this information:

  house address and name of street
  name of city, state, and ZIP code
  month, date, and year

Follow these punctuation and capitalization rules.

1. Capitalize all proper names.
2. Place a comma between the name of the city and the state.
3. Use the correct ZIP code.
4. Place a comma between the date and the year.

Writing the Heading In your best handwriting, write this heading correctly. Follow the punctuation and capitalization rules above. Use a separate sheet of paper.

1509 riverside drive
tulsa oklahoma 74119
august 20 1987

1509 Riverside Drive
Tulsa, Oklahoma 74119
August 20, 1987

Skills Practice Book, Aqua Level
Copyright © by McDougal, Littell & Company

The Parts of a Friendly Letter (2)

Writing a Letter 163

The second part of a friendly letter, after the heading, is the greeting. The **greeting** is how you say "hello." Write the greeting below the heading at the left margin. Here are some examples:

Dear Mrs. Harrington,   Hello, Glenn,

Follow these punctuation and capitalization rules:

1. Capitalize the first word and any proper nouns.
2. Capitalize titles such as *Dr., Mrs., Mr., Ms.,* and *Miss.*
3. Use a period to abbreviate titles like *Dr., Mrs., Mr.,* and *Ms.*
4. Use a comma after the greeting.

The **body** is where you talk to your friend. Write the body below the greeting. Indent the first line of every paragraph.

The **closing** is a simple way of saying "goodbye." Write the closing one line below the body. Line it up with the first word of the heading. Here are some examples of closings:

Your friend,   Sincerely,   With love,

Capitalize only the first word in the closing. Use a comma after the closing.

The **signature** is your handwritten name. Write it below the closing. Line it up with the first word in the closing. If you do not know the reader well, use your entire name.

Writing Friendly Letters In your best handwriting, copy the following parts of a letter. Use correct capitalization and punctuation.

1. dear dr kirk

   Dear Dr. Kirk,

2. dear mike

   Dear Mike,

3. sincerely yours

   Sincerely yours,

4. your niece

   Your niece,

5. yours truly

   Yours truly,

Writing Invitations

Writing Letters
164

Invitations should give information to answer these questions:

1. What kind of activity is it?
2. Why is the activity taking place?
3. Where will the activity be held?
4. When will the activity be held? Tell the day, date, and time.

> 720 Oak Lane SW
> Tacoma, Washington 98499
> June 30, 1987
>
> Dear Kenneth,
>   You are invited to a cookout at my house. It will be on Friday, the Fourth of July, at 5:00 P.M. After we eat, we will walk to the park and watch the fireworks.
>
>   Your friend,
>   Morgan

Writing Invitations Write an invitation for one of the following events. **Invitations will vary.**

1. Ask a friend to a Halloween party.
2. Ask your parents to an Open House at school.

Writing Thank-you Notes

Thank-you notes show that you like what someone did for you. Here are some times you may want to write thank-you notes:

1. When you receive a gift
2. When you have been a guest
3. When someone has done a favor for you

Always write thank-you notes as soon as possible.

Thank-you notes are short. The heading may be shortened to just the date.

August 5, 1987

Dear Wendy,

Thank you for watering my garden while I was on vacation. All of my vegetables look healthy. I will give you some tomatoes when they are ripe.

Sincerely yours,
Sara

Writing Thank-you Notes Write a thank-you note for one of the following reasons. Write neatly. **Thank-you notes will vary.**

1. Thank your uncle for a birthday gift.
2. Thank a neighbor for having you as a guest for dinner.

Writing Business Letters (1)

Writing Letters
166

The parts of a business letter are similar to the parts of a friendly letter. However, a business letter is more formal. Also, a business letter has one added part, the inside address.

> **Heading**
> 329 Hollins Road, NE
> Roanoke, Virginia, 24019
> April 16, 1987
>
> **Inside Address**
> New Hampshire Vacation Center
> P.O. Box 856
> Concord, New Hampshire 03301
>
> **Greeting**
> Dear Sir or Madam:
>
> **Body**
> My family will be visiting your state this summer. Please send me your "Calendar of Events" by May 1 so that we can make our vacation plans. Thank you very much.
>
> **Closing** Sincerely yours,
> **Signature** Martin Joyce
> Martin Joyce

The **inside address** is the address of the company to which you are writing. It is the same as the address on the envelope. Write the inside address below the heading, at the left margin.

The **greeting** should be formal. If you do not know the name of the person to whom you are writing, use one of the following:

Dear Sir or Madam:
Dear Ladies and Gentlemen:

Write the greeting one space below the inside address. Use a colon (:) at the end of the greeting.

Beginning a Business Letter Write the heading, inside address, and greeting of a business letter from you to the principal of your school. Use a separate sheet of paper.

Writing Business Letters (2)

The **body** of a business letter should be short. Include these details:

1. What you are writing about
2. Why you need this information
3. When you need this information.

The **closing** should be formal. Here are samples:

Very truly yours,   Sincerely,   Respectfully,

The **signature** should include your full name. Print your name under your signature.

The **envelope** for a business letter follows the same rules as for a friendly letter.

Writing a Business Letter Write a business letter to: Ms. Stella Rey, Outworld Vacations Company, 9 Crater Drive, Luna City, Moon 99999. Your class would like to take a field trip to the moon. Ask for a list of tourist attractions and their prices. Use your school address as the return address. **Letters will vary.**

_____

_____

_____

Ms. Stella Rey_____

Outworld Vacations Company____

9 Crater Drive_____

Luna City, Moon 99999_____

_____

_____

_____

_____

_____

_____

_____

Addressing the Envelope

Writing Letters 168

The envelope has two different addresses:

1. The address of the person to whom you are writing
2. Your address, called the **return** address

When you address an envelope, follow these steps:

1. Begin the address in the center of the envelope.
2. Put your return address in the upper left-hand corner.
3. Double-check all numbers in the address.

Return Address

Karen Green
2310 Taylor Road
Canyon, Texas 79015

Address

Ms. Linda Brink
141 Washington Avenue
Albany, New York 12245

Addressing an Envelope Address the envelope below to the following address: Mr. James Stimson, 18 Ridge Road, Concord, Maine 01742. Use your own address for the return address.

(Return Address)

Mr. James Stimson
18 Ridge Road
Concord, Maine 01742

Review: Writing Letters

Identifying the Parts of a Letter Answer the questions below.

1. The business letter has one part that the friendly letter does not.

    What is that part? __**inside address**__

2. What are the five parts that both friendly letters and business letters have?

    __**heading**__ __**closing**__

    __**greeting**__ __**signature**__

    __**body**__

3. Write the greeting for both a friendly letter and a business letter.
    You are writing to Dr. Bennett.

    (friendly) __**Dear Dr. Bennett,**__   (business) __**Dear Dr. Bennett:**__

4. Write the heading for a letter. Use this information:
    1234 Park Place, Monopoly, New York 10018, today's date.

    __**1234 Park Place**__

    __**Monopoly, New York 10018**__

    __**(today's date)**__

5. Address the business envelope below. Use your name and address for the return address. Address the envelope to President James Madison, 1600 Pennsylvania Avenue, Washington, D.C. 20013.

(return address)

    President James Madison
    1600 Pennsylvania Avenue
    Washington, D.C. 20013

Practice Pages on Irregular Verbs

Most verbs that tell about the past add *-ed* to the basic form of the verb. These verbs are called **regular verbs.** Some verbs change their entire form to tell about the past. These verbs that show past time in different ways are called **irregular verbs.**

The exercise below will help you find which irregular verbs give you problems. Then you can do the exercise pages on those verbs.

Pretest: Using Irregular Verbs

Read these sentences. Choose the correct verb form in the parentheses. Then underline the correct verb form.

1. Jean has (bring, brought) her new skates.
2. Pat's father (came, come) to drive her home.
3. Have you (did, done) your homework?
4. Marianne (went, gone) to Chicago.
5. Val has (ran, run) two miles today.
6. Sue has (ate, eaten) three large pickles.
7. José had (gave, given) Sam a red pencil.
8. We just (saw, seen) the talent show.
9. Ray has not (took, taken) the spelling test.
10. Michael (threw, thrown) the ball to Katie.

Hear It Right   Say It Right

Irregular Verbs
171

Listen as someone reads these sentences. Listen to the sound of *brought*. Take turns. Read the sentences aloud.

BRING
BROUGHT
BROUGHT

1. Has anyone *brought* in the groceries?
2. Dad *brought* me to school today.
3. Leo *had brought* his camera to the zoo.
4. Mandy's double *brought* in two runs.
5. *Have* you *brought* a pencil?
6. Luckily, we *brought* an umbrella.

> Use *brought* alone, without a helping verb.
> Use *brought* with the helping verbs *is, are, was, were, has, have,* and *had*.

Write It Right

Read these sentences. Write the correct form of *bring* in the blank.

1. I wish I had __**brought**__ my sweater.
2. Both boys were __**brought**__ to the doctor.
3. Everyone __**brought**__ prizes for the grab bag.
4. Who hasn't __**brought**__ a raincoat?
5. The waitress had __**brought**__ our salads.
6. Sam __**brought**__ his dog to school yesterday.
7. The builders have __**brought**__ their tools.
8. Mom __**brought**__ home a cream pie.
9. Pioneers __**brought**__ all they owned with them.
10. Has anyone __**brought**__ a can opener?

Hear It Right   Say It Right

Irregular Verbs
172

Listen as someone reads these sentences. Listen to the sound of *came* and *come*. Take turns. Read the sentences aloud.

COME
CAME
COME

1. A crowd *came* out to see the parade.
2. My cousins *have come* to visit.
3. Joe *came* to school early.
4. The plane from Detroit *has* not *come* yet.
5. Linda *came* to the picnic.
6. The letter *had* never *come*.

> Use *came* alone, without a helping verb.
> Use *come* with the helping verbs *has, have,* and *had*.

Write It Right

Read these sentences. Choose the correct form of the verb in parentheses. Then underline the correct verb form.

1. The whistle (<u>came</u>, come) in a cereal box.
2. The Jacksons had (came, <u>come</u>) for dinner.
3. My aunt has (came, <u>come</u>) for the weekend.
4. This vase (<u>came</u>, come) from China.
5. The pizza has finally (came, <u>come</u>).
6. The players have (came, <u>come</u>) onto the field.
7. My grandparents (<u>came</u>, come) here from Japan.
8. Your brother has (came, <u>come</u>) for you.
9. Has anyone (came, <u>come</u>) to fix the stove?
10. Everyone (<u>came</u>, come) on time.

Irregular Verbs

Hear It Right Say It Right

Listen as someone reads these sentences. Listen to the sound of *did* and *done*. Take turns. Read the sentences aloud.

DO
DID
DONE

1. Patty *did* a cartwheel on the lawn.
2. I *had done* my best to help Carl.
3. What *was done* about the flat tire?
4. We *did* the dishes quickly.
5. Who *did* that drawing?
6. Ken *has done* good work.

> Use *did* alone, without a helping verb.
> Use *done* with the helping verbs *is, are, was, were, has, have,* and *had.*

Write It Right

Read these sentences. Choose the correct form of the verb in parentheses. Then underline the correct verb form.

1. Our class (<u>did</u>, done) a circus mural.
2. We had never (did, <u>done</u>) one before.
3. Mike has not (did, <u>done</u>) anything wrong.
4. You (<u>did</u>, done) a good job on that map.
5. What has Willy (did, <u>done</u>) with the football?
6. Cindy (<u>did</u>, done) a jigsaw puzzle.
7. Jill has (did, <u>done</u>) some weeding today.
8. Everyone (<u>did</u>, done) well on the test.
9. What have you (did, <u>done</u>) with this problem?
10. Sheila (<u>did</u>, done) twenty sit-ups in gym class.

Hear It Right   Say It Right

Irregular Verbs
174

Listen as someone reads these sentences. Listen to the sound of *ate* and *eaten*. Take turns. Read the sentences aloud.

EAT
ATE
EATEN

1. The hamster *has eaten* all its food.
2. Lee *ate* my peanut butter sandwich.
3. I *ate* breakfast very early this morning.
4. *Have* you ever *eaten* figs?
5. The squirrels *had eaten* all our bread.
6. Carrots, tomatoes, and peppers *are eaten* raw or cooked.

> Use *ate* alone, without a helping verb.
> Use *eaten* with the helping verbs *is, are, was, were, has, have,* and *had*.

Write It Right

Read these sentences. Choose the correct form of the verb in parentheses. Then underline the correct verb form.

1. Harold (<u>ate</u>, eaten) four pancakes.
2. What have you (ate, <u>eaten</u>) for dinner?
3. Someone has (ate, <u>eaten</u>) all the nuts.
4. Pam (<u>ate</u>, eaten) at the counter.
5. Adele had never (ate, <u>eaten</u>) tacos before.
6. We often (<u>ate</u>, eaten) our meals on the porch.
7. Has Dad (ate, <u>eaten</u>) lunch yet?
8. I had (ate, <u>eaten</u>) too many grapes.
9. The goats (<u>ate</u>, eaten) the leaves off the bush.
10. The cherries were (ate, <u>eaten</u>) by birds.

Hear It Right   Say It Right

Irregular Verbs
175

Listen as someone reads these sentences. Listen to the sound of *gave* and *given*. Take turns. Read the sentences aloud.

GIVE
GAVE
GIVEN

1. Ida *gave* her place in line to me.
2. Who *has given* me this cold?
3. Terry *has given* away his old sled.
4. Every year, an award *is given* for service to the school.
5. Judy *gave* all her peanuts to the elephant.
6. The clerk *had given* us the wrong change.

> Use *gave* alone, without a helping verb.
> Use *given* with the helping verbs *is, are, was, were, have, has,* and *had.*

Write It Right

Read these sentences. Choose the correct form of the verb in parentheses. Then underline the correct verb form.

1. Who (<u>gave</u>, given) Billy that kitten?
2. The noise has (gave, <u>given</u>) Mom a headache.
3. Todd has (gave, <u>given</u>) his book away.
4. Many generous people (<u>gave</u>, given) to UNICEF.
5. Andy was (gave, <u>given</u>) two free tickets.
6. We (<u>gave</u>, given) a birthday party for Ms. Lopez.
7. Alex has (gave, <u>given</u>) me some good advice.
8. Becky (<u>gave</u>, given) a talk about rubber.
9. The jury was (gave, <u>given</u>) a five-minute break.
10. I (<u>gave</u>, given) half of my sandwich to Shelly.

Hear It Right   Say It Right

Listen as someone reads these sentences. Listen to the sound of *went* and *gone*. Take turns. Read the sentences aloud.

GO
WENT
GONE

1. I *went* to the movie with my sister.
2. Meg *has gone* to a tennis game.
3. That car *went* through a red light.
4. *Have* you ever *gone* to Disney World?
5. All of the milk *is gone*.
6. Every light in the house *had gone* out.

> Use *went* alone, without a helping verb.
> Use *gone* with the helping verbs *is, are, was, were, have, has,* and *had.*

Write It Right

Read these sentences. Choose the correct form of the verb in parentheses. Then underline the correct verb form.

1. Mary (<u>went</u>, gone) into her bedroom.
2. Everyone has (went, <u>gone</u>) to the park.
3. Has anyone (went, <u>gone</u>) to get Sam?
4. Carol had (went, <u>gone</u>) to the party early.
5. Hank has (went, <u>gone</u>) to sleep.
6. Ed (<u>went</u>, gone) shopping with Aunt Helen.
7. Most robins have (went, <u>gone</u>) south.
8. Marvin has never (went, <u>gone</u>) to a rodeo.
9. Who (<u>went</u>, gone) with you on the boat ride?
10. The explorers (<u>went</u>, gone) into the cave.

Hear It Right Say It Right

Irregular Verbs

● Listen as someone reads these sentences. Listen to the sound of *ran* and *run*. Take turns. Read the sentences aloud.

RUN
RAN
RUN

1. Debbie *ran* for class president.
2. *Have* you ever *run* a hundred-meter dash?
3. David *ran* slowly up the hill.
4. The sack race *was run* last.
5. Smokey *ran* after a squirrel.
6. That clock *has* never *run* on time.

Use *ran* alone, without a helping verb.
Use *run* with the helping verbs *is, are, was, were, has, have,* and *had.*

Write It Right

Read these sentences. Choose the correct form of the verb in parentheses. Then underline the correct verb form.

●
1. This pen has (ran, <u>run</u>) out of ink.
2. Leon had (ran, <u>run</u>) for help.
3. The gray horse (<u>ran</u>, run) the fastest.
4. The movie was (ran, <u>run</u>) backwards.
5. Martha's dad has (ran, <u>run</u>) in a marathon.
6. Richard (<u>ran</u>, run) after his dog.
7. Have you ever (ran, <u>run</u>) a mile?
8. The lifeguard (<u>ran</u>, run) in three races.
9. Mrs. Kent once (<u>ran</u>, run) a grocery store.
10. The stalled truck (<u>ran</u>, run) out of gas.

Hear It Right   Say It Right

Irregular Verbs
178

Listen as someone reads these sentences. Listen to the sound of *seen* and *saw*. Take turns. Read the sentences aloud.

SEE
SAW
SEEN

1. No one *saw* me leave the room.
2. *Has* anyone *seen* the basketball?
3. Dad *had* never *seen* so much traffic.
4. I just *saw* Gerry yesterday.
5. Bears *are* often *seen* in Yellowstone Park.
6. *Have* you ever *seen* a tumbleweed?

> Use *saw* alone, without a helping verb.
> Use *seen* with the helping verbs *is, are, was, were, have, has,* and *had*.

Write It Right

Read these sentences. Choose the correct form of the verb in parentheses. Then underline the correct verb form.

1. Sarah has (saw, <u>seen</u>) all these magic tricks before.
2. Have you ever (saw, <u>seen</u>) so many people?
3. The guests (<u>saw</u>, seen) Mr. Whitman's slides of Alaska.
4. A red glow was (saw, <u>seen</u>) in the sky.
5. Who (<u>saw</u>, seen) Mrs. Gold this morning?
6. I have (saw, <u>seen</u>) only one other boy here.
7. The travelers had never (saw, <u>seen</u>) a desert storm.
8. Viewers (<u>saw</u>, seen) the hurricane on the news.
9. Carlos once (<u>saw</u>, seen) a shooting star.
10. No one had (saw, <u>seen</u>) the videotape of the party.

Irregular Verbs
179

Hear It Right   Say It Right

Listen as someone reads these sentences. Listen to the sound of *took* and *taken*. Take turns. Read the sentences aloud.

TAKE
TOOK
TAKEN

1. Mom *took* Uncle Bob to the airport.
2. *Have* you *taken* the dog for a walk?
3. Who *took* my ruler?
4. Dad *had taken* Jimmy to the doctor.
5. Ann *took* a close look at the turtle.
6. All the good seats *were taken*.

> Use *took* alone, without a helping verb.
> Use *taken* with the helping verbs *is, are, was, were, have, has,* and *had.*

Write It Right

Read these sentences. Choose the correct form of the verb in parentheses. Then underline the correct verb form.

1. I have never (took, <u>taken</u>) swimming lessons.
2. Jay (<u>took</u>, taken) his bike to the shop for repairs.
3. Has Cathy (took, <u>taken</u>) her medicine?
4. This painting has (took, <u>taken</u>) first prize.
5. Stan (<u>took</u>, taken) my picture near the gate.
6. The coats were (took, <u>taken</u>) to the cleaners.
7. We have (took, <u>taken</u>) this bus before.
8. Ms. Jenks (<u>took</u>, taken) the train to work.
9. Ned has (took, <u>taken</u>) his letter to the post office.
10. Janet (<u>took</u>, taken) the message to Mrs. Blair.

Hear It Right Say It Right

Irregular Verbs
180

Listen as someone reads these sentences. Listen to the sound of *threw* and *thrown*. Take turns. Read the sentences aloud.

THROW
THREW
THROWN

1. Laurie *threw* the winning basket.
2. The rider *was thrown* from his horse.
3. Few pitchers *have* ever *thrown* a no-hitter.
4. The players *threw* their hats in the air.
5. The quarterback *has thrown* another touchdown.
6. We *have thrown* our litter into the barrel.

> Use *threw* alone, without a helping verb.
> Use *thrown* with the helping verbs *is, are, was, were, has, have,* and *had*.

Write It Right

Read these sentences. Choose the correct form of the verb in parentheses. Then underline the correct verb form.

1. Tom (<u>threw</u>, thrown) his fastest pitch.
2. Have you (threw, <u>thrown</u>) out the funnies?
3. José had (threw, <u>thrown</u>) the Frisbee.
4. The girls (<u>threw</u>, thrown) snowballs at us.
5. The tourist (<u>threw</u>, thrown) a penny into the well.
6. Confetti was (threw, <u>thrown</u>) into the air.
7. Sharon had (threw, <u>thrown</u>) away the stale bread.
8. Grampa has (threw, <u>thrown</u>) out crumbs for the birds.
9. Who (<u>threw</u>, thrown) that paper airplane?
10. The bucking bronco had (threw, <u>thrown</u>) its rider.

Adding Prefixes and Certain Suffixes

Adding Prefixes A **prefix** is a syllable that is added to the beginning of a word to change its meaning. **When you add a prefix to a word, the spelling of the word stays the same.**

PREFIX	BASE WORD	NEW WORD
re- (again)	paint	repaint (paint again)
dis- (not)	honest	dishonest (not honest)
un- (not)	real	unreal (not real)
in- (not)	sincere	insincere (not sincere)
im- (not)	polite	impolite (not polite)
pre- (before)	view	preview (view before)
mis- (incorrectly)	spell	misspell (spell incorrectly)

Adding Suffixes A **suffix** is a letter or syllable added to the ending of a word to form a new word.

When you add the suffix -ly to a word ending with l, you keep both l's.

careful + ly = carefully   usual + ly = usually

When you add the suffix -ness to a word ending with n, you keep both n's.

mean + ness = meanness   stubborn + ness = stubbornness

Adding Prefixes and Suffixes Add the prefix or suffix given for each word. Write the new word on the line.

1. re + pay = **repay**
2. un + able = **unable**
3. dis + obey = **disobey**
4. un + named = **unnamed**
5. im + movable = **immovable**
6. pre + judge = **prejudge**
7. mis + behave = **misbehave**
8. real + ly = **really**
9. even + ness = **evenness**
10. gradual + ly = **gradually**

Words Ending in Silent e and y

When you add a suffix beginning with a vowel to a word ending in silent e, you usually drop the final e.

    change + ing = changing   safe + er = safer

When you add a suffix beginning with a consonant to a word ending in silent e, you usually keep the final e.

    move + ment = movement   safe + ly = safely

The following words are exceptions:

    truly   argument   ninth   judgment

When you add a suffix to a word that ends with y following a consonant, you usually change the y to i. Do not change the y when the suffix -ing is added.

    scary + est = scariest   easy + ly = easily
    fry + ing = frying   carry + ing = carrying

When you add a suffix to a word that ends with y following a vowel, you usually keep the y.

    enjoy + ment = enjoyment   joy + ful = joyful

The following words are exceptions: **paid, said.**

Adding Suffixes Correctly
Add the suffix. Write the new word correctly.

1. dine + ing = **dining**
2. write + er = **writer**
3. sure + ly = **surely**
4. lone + ly = **lonely**
5. argue + ment = **argument**
6. copy + ed = **copied**
7. friendly + ness = **friendliness**
8. cry + ing = **crying**
9. stay + ing = **staying**
10. say + ed = **said**

Doubling the Final Consonant and Spelling Words with *ie* and *ei*

Words of one syllable, ending with a consonant following one vowel, double the final consonant before adding -*ing*, -*ed*, -*er*, or -*est*.

tan + ing = tanning   hop + ed = hopped
hot + er = hotter   big + est = biggest

The final consonant is not doubled when it follows two vowels.

scream + ing = screaming   cool + er = cooler

Spelling Words with *ie* and *ei* The rule is found in this rhyme:

I before *e*
Except after *c*,
Or when sounded as *a*
As in n*ei*ghbor or w*ei*gh.

These words follow the rules:

friend   receive   eight   chief

These words are exceptions:

either   neither   seize   weird

Using the Spelling Rules Underline the misspelled word in each sentence. Spell it correctly on the line.

1. Judy is a good <u>swimer</u>.   **swimmer**

2. The Scouts <u>planed</u> a camping trip.   **planned**

3. Ron <u>needded</u> a stamp for his letter.   **needed**

4. Kurt <u>stired</u> the soup.   **stirred**

5. Nancy <u>leapped</u> across the puddle.   **leaped**

6. The Joyces painted <u>thier</u> house.   **their**

7. I do not <u>beleive</u> in ghosts.   **believe**

8. Robin <u>recieved</u> a package in the mail.   **received**

9. The wind made a <u>wierd</u> sound.   **weird**

10. Terry cut the cake into ten <u>peices</u>.   **pieces**